Equity and Trusts Law 2020/2021 -

Simply Notes

CONTENTS

WHAT IS THIS BOOK?

1. It is a simple and straightforward introduction to equity and trusts law.

2. It is an up-to-date set of law subject notes.

3. It is a book designed to give you a quick and accessible knowledge of the law in a particular area of your course of study, before you move on to more complex texts.

4. It is suitable for students studying LLB, GDL, LLM/MA law conversion courses, PGDL, or CILEx qualifications.

5. It is a book which is not a replacement for hard work and dedication to the programme of study you have embarked on.

CHAPTER 1
INTRODUCTION TO EQUITY AND
THE TRUST CONCEPT

Introduction

1.01 This book is about equity and the law of trusts. Equity is a jurisdiction which grew, to a degree, out of dissatisfaction with the common law. This chapter is about the fundamentals: what is equity? What is a trust?

Equity

1.02 It would be easy to think of equity as 'fairness', but it is more complex than that term. Equity is a body of law and rules whose origins lie in the complexities of the common law system. Equity gave birth to many modern remedies, and arguably its most significant contribution to English law: the trust.

Historical development of equity

1.03 A system of law common to England was developed after the Norman Conquest. This common law had, by the mid-thirteenth century, become strict and rigid as the writs needed to issue new claims were not available. The litigant, disappointed with their treatment at common law, would appeal directly to the Monarch to resolve disputes.

1.04 Gradually, over time, the Monarch passed matters to the Lord Chancellor for determination and, by the fifteenth century, a separate court had been established to hear those claims: the Chancery. These decisions gradually became the body of law which we know today as equity.

1.05 This meant that the English legal system had two bodies of law operating side-by-side, determining on similar factual

1

disputes: common law and equity. This created a conflict which was resolved in favour of equity by the **Earl of Oxford's Case (1615)**, which was enshrined in s25(11), Judicature Act 1873.

Basis of Equitable Jurisdiction

1.06 The basis for decisions made by the Lord Chancellor in Chancery was **conscience**. Lord Chancellors were not legally trained, they were clerics, ie, priests. Consequently, decisions could not be based on law.

1.07 The conscience basis for decisions brought criticism that decisions of Chancery were unpredictable. John Selden famously commented that equity varied with the length of the Chancellor's foot. In other words, decisions altered as each Lord Chancellor was replaced.

1.08 In response to this criticism, successive Lord Chancellors sought to formalize decision-making in equity. This was achieved by a more principled approach to decisions through the **maxims of equity**.

Maxims of Equity

Equity will not suffer a wrong to be without a remedy	No wrong should be allowed to go without remedy if it is capable of being remedied by a court
Equity follows the law	Where law provides an answer to the legal issue before the courts, equity will follow the law, coming to the same conclusion
Where there is equal equity, the law shall prevail	Where the parties have equal equities, so neither has a better claim than the other, the legal answer shall prevail to remedy the dispute

Where the equities are equal, the first in time shall prevail	Where there are two competing equitable claims to a property, then the first of the two is the better of the two
He who seeks equity must do equity	Where a party seeks equitable relief, they must be prepared to perform their duties towards the other party
He who comes to equity must come with clean hands	A party seeking the intervention of equity, must have "clean hands", ie, have behaved in good conscience in the action for resolution
Delay defeats equity	Any party wishing the intervention of equity should not delay the claim unduly for they may lose the right to bring the claim
Equality is equity	This is not always to be taken literally, but rather seen as a sentiment that a court of equity should operate in an even-handed manner between the parties
Equity looks to the intent rather than the form	Equity is not concerned whether the correct procedure has been followed, rather it is more concerned to ensure that the claimant's intention was clear
Equity looks on that as done which ought to be done	Equity looks upon the matter as complete, even though the full formalities of a transaction are not complete

Equity imputes an intention to fulfil an obligation	Where the parties have an express of inferred intention, equity will intervene to see that obligation is fulfilled by the parties
Equity acts in personam	Equity acts against the conscience of the individual

1.09 The maxims retain some residual relevance today, though the modern approach is to rely on binding precedent.

1.10 All this aside, equity's most significant contribution to English private law is the trust, and the bulk of this book is concerned with explaining the trust concept.

Origins of the Trust

1.11 At common law, title to land was proved by holding seisin. If the holder had title, common law recognised that right and enforced it. When fighting overseas, the holder of land would transfer title to a trusted friend to look after the land while they were away. This would often be coupled with an instruction to hold the land for a family member, usually a son, should the man not return from battle.

1.12 In some circumstances, the trusted friend who had been given title would, on the death of his friend, deny any such obligation. The disappointed party, the son, would not be able to prove ownership because they would not have title, so instead would appeal to equity and the Monarch or Lord Chancellor would recognise the right possessed of the son. This would be an equitable right.

1.13 This idea of there being two forms of ownership in the same piece of land is the basis of the trust. One person, who became the **trustee**, would have **legal title**; the other person, who became the **beneficiary**, would have **equitable title**. This is fundamental to the trust; separation of title.

The Trust Concept

1.14 A trust is an **equitable obligation** where **legal title is given to the trustee** and **equitable title is held by the beneficiary**. Equitable title is also known as the beneficial title.

1.15 The three parties to a settlement on trust are the **settlor**, who **creates the trust**, the **trustee**, who **administers the trust**, and the **beneficiary**, who takes the **benefit of the trust**.

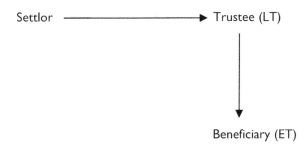

1.16 This diagram illustrates the traditional **settlement on trust**, ie, the settlor and trustee are different people. In a **self-declaration** of trust, the **settlor and trustee would be the same person. The trustee has legal title ('LT'), while the beneficiary has equitable title ('ET')**.

1.17 Under the usual settlement on trust in the diagram, once the trust is created, the settlor drops from the picture; he has no further role to play in the trust.

1.18 We have seen that a settlor may make himself a trustee; equally, the settlor may make himself a beneficiary, with a different person as the trustee.

1.19 When the trust is created, separate ownership is created; legal owner with legal title, equitable owner with equitable title. It is important to understand the equitable title is a property right and it gives the holder the right to do with the equitable interest as they like. For example, the beneficiary could sell the equitable interest, or give it away.

Categories of Trust

1.20 At a basic level, there are **two types of trust**: **express** and **implied** trusts. These can be further separated into:

Express Trust	Implied Trust
1. Private trusts for people 2. Private trusts for purposes 3. Public trusts for purposes (charitable trusts)	1. Resulting trusts 2. Constructive trusts

1.21 Broadly, express trusts are expressly created by the settlor, whereas implied trusts are imposed by law as a response to certain circumstances.

Types of Trust

1.22 There are a number of different trust types: **Fixed Trusts**, **Discretionary Trusts**, **Successive Interest Trusts**, and **Protective Trusts**.

1.23 A **fixed trust** is one where the obligation is fixed by the settlor. An example would be 'to my trustee to hold for A and B *equally*'. Here, the obligation is fixed for the trustee; the property is to be held equally between the beneficiaries. Here, the interests of the parties are **concurrent**; they exist at the same time.

1.24 A **discretionary trust** is one where the trustee is given a discretion as to distribution of the trust property. An example would be, 'to my trustee to distribute between A and B as you in your *absolute discretion shall select*'. In the example, the trustee has a discretion as to distribution between A and B.

1.25 A discretionary trust may be **exhaustive** or **non-exhaustive**. An exhaustive discretionary trust requires the trustee to distribute the income from the trust when it arises within a reasonable time. A non-exhaustive trust allows trustees the power to accumulate. In other words, a non-exhaustive discretionary trust does not require the income to be distributed every year.

1.26 A **successive interest trust** is one where the beneficiaries enjoy their interests one after the other. An example would be 'to my trustee to hold for A for life, remainder to B.' Here the interests are **successive** because A has their interest first, and B their interest afterwards.

1.27 A **protective trust** arises where the settlor leaves property 'on protective trust' and s33, Trustee Act 1925 takes over. A protective trust, as its name suggests, seeks to protect the beneficiary from his own failings. Under a protective trust, the **principal beneficiary has a life interest**. If declared **bankrupt**, or attempts to dispose of their life interest, the interest automatically ends and is replaced with a discretionary trust of the income for the rest of the principal beneficiary's life. The discretionary trust becomes a trust for the benefit of the principal beneficiary, their spouse, and children of the principal beneficiary.

Trusts Terminology

1.28 You will encounter significant terminology in equity and trusts, so it is wise to familiarise yourself with it.

Income	Income is the sum which is generated from the trust fund. Thus, if the trust fund consists of a house, the income generated by it might be rent which is paid by a tenant. Alternatively, if the trust fund consists of shares, then the income would be a dividend declared on those shares.
Capital	Capital is whatever comprises the trust fund. It might be funds deposited with a bank, or a house, or a block of shares.
Life interest	A life interest, as its name suggests, is an interest which the beneficiary enjoys for their life. When they die, the interest dies with them; they cannot leave it under their will. The holder of the life interest has an interest in income.
Remainder interest	The remainder interest is the interest which follows the life interest. After the person with the life interest dies, the beneficiary entitled then takes the 'remainder interest'.
Life tenant	The beneficiary who holds the 'life interest'.
Remainderman	The beneficiary who holds the 'remainder interest'.

Vested interest	A vested interest is one which is enjoyed without conditions attached to it. For example, 'to A for life, remainder to B'. Both interests here are vested because neither A nor B has to do anything for the interest to vest. In this example, we say that A has an interest vested in possession; vested in now. B has an interest which is vested in interest; vested in the future.
Contingent interest	A contingent interest is one which will only be enjoyed once a condition is satisfied. For example, 'to A for life, remainder to B if B survives A'. A's interest is vested, but B's interest is contingent because he has to outlive A.

The Rule in Saunders v Vautier

1.29 The rule in **Saunders v Vautier (1841)** allows the beneficiary to bring the trust to an end, and operates irrespective of the settlor's wishes.

1.30 The **conditions** are that the **beneficiary must be absolutely entitled**, and of **full age** and **sound mind**. In such circumstances, he calls for legal title and the trust comes to an end. Where legal and equitable title are in the hands of the same person, the trust comes to an end.

1.31 The rule in Saunders v Vautier also applies to trusts with multiple beneficiaries. They must be **together absolutely entitled** and all of full age and sound mind.

Gifts and Powers

1.32 It is also important to understand other concepts, namely the **gift** and the **power**.

1.33 A gift is the transfer of legal and equitable ownership in property to the transferee. The person making the gift is the donor, the recipient is the donee. Whether a gift or trust is meant depends on **intention**.

1.34 A power is the ability, but not the obligation, to do something. For example, trustees have the power to insure the trust property but do not have to do so. Of course, in most cases that would be sensible! There are different categories of power.

Personal power	A personal power is given to someone who is not a trustee. For example, a beneficiary with a life interest (a life tenant) might be give the power to determine the destination of the capital.
Fiduciary power	A fiduciary power is given to a trustee. For example, a trustee might be given the power to add to the class of beneficiaries making up the class.
General power	A general power may be exercised in favour of anybody in the world.
Special power	A special power may be exercised in favour of a limited class.
Hybrid power	A hybrid power may be

	exercised in favour of anybody in the world, subject to excluded persons.

Trusts and Powers compared

1.35 Trusts and powers can, in some circumstances, operate in a very similar manner. In the table below is an indication of how trusts and powers compare.

Trusts	Powers
A trust is an obligation which must be performed.	A power is the ability to do something and does not have to be performed.
A trust can be enforced.	A power cannot be enforced.
The rule in Saunders v Vautier applies to trusts.	The rule in Saunders v Vautier does not apply to powers.

CHAPTER 2
THE 'THREE CERTAINTIES'

Introduction

2.01 All express private trusts in English law should comply with the three certainties (**Knight v Knight (1840)**). The settlor must show that he is clear that he wants to create a trust (certainty of intention), clear what property is to be held on trust (certainty of subject-matter), and clear who the beneficiaries are under the trust (certainty of objects). If one of the certainties is missing, the trust is void.

Rationale for the 'Three Certainties'

2.02 It is imperative that the settlor satisfy the three certainties since the trustee should know the extent of the obligation imposed upon him. If there is any degree of uncertainty, for example, as to who the beneficiary is and the trustee distributes the trust to the wrong person, the trustee is personally liable for a breach of trust. Additionally, if the court is called upon to carry out the trust in the event of the trustee's default or death, the court also needs to understand the extent of the obligation. So, certainty is paramount in the creation of an express private trust in English law.

Certainty of Intention

2.03 The settlor has to intend to create a trust, as opposed to a gift or some other transfer of property. The intention to create a trust can come from the words used, or from the settlor's conduct. The words may be written or spoken, but whichever is the case the words need to be imperative, imposing an obligation, and not precatory, which only expresses a hope or a wish.

Certainty of Intention: Written word

2.04 Traditionally, trusts were created formally by a professionally drafted trust deed. The court would then be called upon to interpret the words in the trust deed to determine whether a trust had been created. Historically, the courts would seek to identify key terms in the trust in order to determine whether a trust is created or not. However, the modern approach is to take the whole document, construing the words, to see what they mean (**Re James (1935)**). This means that trust deeds with similar phrases may or may not create a trust depending on the wider context in which the words are used. For example, two cases which are often compared are **Re Adams and the Kensington Vestry (1884)** and **Comiskey v Bowring-Hanbury (1905)**. In both cases, the phrase 'in full confidence' was used in the context of a professionally drafted trust deed, but in only one was a trust created.

2.05 In **Re Adams and the Kensington Vestry (1884)**, the testator left his estate to the use of his wife in full confidence that she would 'do what is right' as to the disposal of it between the children, either in her lifetime or in her will after her death. The Court of Appeal held that the wording was precatory, so a trust was not created, the wife taking the property absolutely. The wording, when read in the whole context of the document, was insufficiently precise to create a trust.

2.06 In contrast, in **Comiskey v Bowring-Hanbury (1905)**, though the words 'in full confidence' were also used, in the broader context of the entire document, the wording was imperative, and created a trust obligation. So, in Comiskey, a husband left his entire estate to his wife in full confidence that would divide it, at her discretion, between their nieces. She could determine it in her lifetime or on her death by will. If she didn't, then the estate was to be divided equally between the nieces. In this case, the words created a trust obligation. Taken in their proper context, a trust was intended because it was clear that the husband wished the nieces to benefit in some way or another. Either the wife would determine it, or the 'equally' default provision would determine it.

Certainty of Intention: Spoken Word and Conduct

2.07 Generally, words spoken, or the conduct of the parties, can be sufficient to create a trust. Naturally, if intention is taken from words spoken or conduct, there will be no trust deed; the trust will be informally created. A good case illustrative of this is **Paul v Constance (1977)**. Mr Constance (C) was estranged, but not divorced from, his wife. He lived with Ms Paul (P). C received compensation for an accident at work and he and P sought to open a joint bank account. The bank manager refused this, so C opened the account in his sole name. On several occasions, C said to P that the money was 'as much hers as his'. In addition, C and P made a series of joint deposits to, and withdrawals from, the account. When C died he had no will and because he was still married to Mrs C, she inherited his estate (Administration of Estates Act 1925). P claimed an interest in the funds in the account. The CA, perhaps being generous to P and the circumstances in which she and C arranged their affairs, held that the multiple statements made by C, together with their joint conduct in relation to the account, meant that P had an interest in the account. C was, in fact, holding the funds in the account on trust for himself and P during his lifetime, so that on his death the funds were split equally between P and Mrs C. Interestingly, C never used the word 'trust', but that did not prevent the finding; equity looks at the intention not the form.

2.08 So, whether the words are written or spoken, it is the context in which they are used which will be crucial. If, when taken in their wider context, it is clear that a trust was intended, the courts will so find.

2.09 However, care must be taken that the wording is clear and that wording which is susceptible of multiple meanings, may not always produce the outcome desired. In **Hilton v Cosnier (2018)**, the High Court declined to find a trust had been created where the owner of a house told his partner that she could live in it for life, but that he was giving it to his grandchildren. While this was not a trust, it was clear that he did not want his partner to have the house outright. Further, after making the statement, the owner of the house had acted inconsistently with his earlier statement, so his conduct undermined the intent in the statement. Of course, there was an additional problem in the case in that it concerned land and a declaration of a trust of land should comply with s53(1)(b), LPA 1925 (see paras 3.06 and 3.07, below), which an oral statement would not.

Certainty of Subject-Matter

2.10 The property which is to be held on trust must also be certain at the date of the trust's creation. Certainty of subject-matter has two elements to it: (i) the property which is to be held on trust must be certain and, (ii) the beneficial entitlement must be certain. It is worth noting that there is overlap between certainty of intention and subject-matter; if the subject-matter is unclear, it is also unclear whether there was intention to create a trust (**Mussoorie Bank v Raynor (1882)**).

Certainty of Subject-Matter: Property to be held on trust

2.11 The property which is to be subject to the trust must be ascertained at the date the trust is created; if not, the trust will be void. Therefore, the 'bulk of my estate' (**Palmer v Simmonds (1854)**) will fail, and likewise a purported transfer of 'the remaining part of what is left [of £300]' (**Sprange v Barnard (1789)**) will also fail. Additionally, failure to segregate assets will result in a failed attempt to create a trust. In **Re London Wine (Shippers) Co Ltd (1986)**, a failure to segregate wine meant claims to unsegregated wine in a company's warehouse failed. Likewise, in **Re Goldcorp (1994)**, with unsegregated gold bullion. However, some bullion had been segregated and claims to the segregated bullion succeeded. In contrast, English law does not hold the same where the property is intangible. In **Hunter v Moss (1994)**, a transfer of 50 of 950 issued shares in a private company owned by the donor was valid, even though the 50 shares had not been segregated. Hunter v Moss was followed in the case of **Re Harvard Securities (1997)**.

Certainty of Subject-Matter: Beneficial entitlement

2.12 The issue of what the beneficiary is to receive is also pertinent. In **Boyce v Boyce (1849)**, a case of unusual facts, the property was certain, but the beneficial entitlement was not. A father left his two houses in Southwold to his two daughters, Charlotte and Maria. Maria was to choose a house first, and the other house would then go to Charlotte. This provision is perfectly valid, if the choice is made. Unfortunately, Maria died before exercising her choice, and the court held that the gift failed.

2.13 Where beneficial entitlement is provided in objective terms, such terms are likely to be valid. Thus, in **Re Golay's WT (1967)** a provision for a 'reasonable income for my housekeeper' was valid. 'Reasonable' is a term which appears frequently throughout civil law, so one with which judges are comfortable. It is suggested, however, that the term 'reasonable' should be measured against a benchmark such as, in this case, a 'housekeeper'. Alternatively, as in Golay itself, the measure will take its guide from the standard of living of the intended beneficiary.

Certainty of Objects

2.14 As a general rule, all express private trusts must have a human beneficiary or beneficiaries. If the beneficiaries are named, then certainty of objects does not generally present problems. Problems only really start when the beneficiaries are identified as a 'class' rather than individually. An example might be: '£200,000 held on trust for the education of such of my relatives as my trustees may, in their discretion, see fit.' In this example, the beneficiaries are not individually identified, rather they are identified as a class, ie, the relatives of the settlor. This then gives rise to the question: What is the test for certainty of objects where beneficiaries are identified as a 'class'? Well, the simple answer is that it depends on whether the trust is fixed or discretionary.

Certainty of Objects: Fixed trusts

2.15 Let's say that the settlor creates the following trust: '£200,000 to be divided equally between my children.' Here, a fixed trust is created. The trustee enjoys no discretion as to distribution; he must simply distribute the fund equally between the settlor's children. In order for this to be valid, the trustee must be able to draw up a **complete list** in order to distribute the fund (**IRC v Broadway Cottages (1955)**). The 'complete list' test, as it is sometimes known, requires two things: (i) conceptual and (ii) evidential certainty. Conceptual certainty requires that the class is defined by an objective term. In this case, the concept, children, is capable of objective definition; children would be the issue of the settlor. Evidential certainty would be satisfied where a complete list is drawn up. Crucially, both conceptual and evidential certainty are needed for a fixed trust to be valid.

Certainty of Objects: Discretionary trusts

2.16 Historically, all trusts, whether fixed or discretionary, adopted the same test for certainty of objects where the beneficiaries were identified by reference to a class. However, this orthodoxy was challenged in the middle of the 20th century by the rise in the use of discretionary trusts by wealthy benefactors seeking to share their wealth with large numbers of people, usually employees or ex-employees of their company. These created a difficulty because the class was often so large that it was impossible to draw up a complete list of beneficiaries to satisfy the 'complete list' test. Take this example: '£500,000 to be held on trust for the education of the employees, ex-employees, directors, ex-directors, their relatives, and dependants, as my trustees shall, in their absolute discretion, determine.' Here, there are several concepts in an extremely large class. Maintaining a complete list of all the possible beneficiaries entitled under this trust would be almost, if not entirely, impossible. Something had to be done. Enter, Lord Wilberforce.

Certainty of Objects: Mcphail v Doulton (1970)(HL)

2.17 A clause very similar to the one described in the previous paragraph was considered in the case of McPhail v Doulton. In the House of Lords, Lord Wilberforce, being acutely aware of applying the 'complete list' test to such a trust, distinguished discretionary trusts and fixed trusts, stating that the former should not use the 'complete list' test. Instead, the **test for certainty of objects in a discretionary trust is the 'any given postulant' test** or, to put it in easier language to understand, **the 'is/is not' test**. Can it be said with certainty of any given individual whether he is or is not within the class of beneficiaries? In order to answer this question, as with class beneficiary clauses in fixed trusts, the concept which defines the class must be certain. Where the test is distinct from the 'list test' is that a complete list of beneficiaries is not needed. So, **the 'is/is not' test needs conceptual certainty**, **not evidential certainty**. After the House of Lords delivered its decision, the case was sent back to the Chancery division for determination on the new law for certainty of objects in discretionary trusts. The case ended back in Court of Appeal as **Re Baden (No2)(1973)**.

Certainty of Objects: Re Baden (No2)(1973)(CA)

2.18 This case is crucial to an understanding of the test set down in McPhail. Unhelpfully, however, the three judges in the Court of Appeal (Sachs, Megaw, and Stamp LJJ) didn't make life easy for generations of law students by delivering three different judgements interpreting Lord Wilberforce's 'is/is not' test. Particularly, the case turned on the applicability of the test to the concept of 'relatives' used in the trust deed.

2.19 Sachs LJ - Emphasised the key role of the concept. Once the concept was established to be clear, if it could not be positively proved that a particular individual was within the class, then they would be deemed to be outside the class. 'Relatives' was a certain concept, defined as 'descent from a common ancestor'.

2.20 Megaw LJ - Came to the conclusion that as long as it could be shown that a substantial number of beneficiaries were within the class, then the trust would be valid. A complete list of the beneficiaries was not necessary. Megaw LJ agreed with Sachs LJ's definition of 'relatives'.

2.21 Stamp LJ - It is often written that Stamp LJ's judgment marks a return to the 'list test', but this is a lazy reading of the judgment. Stamp LJ makes it clear that a complete list of beneficiaries is not required, rather that in order to satisfy the 'is/is not' test, it must be shown of any given individual whether *he is or is not* a member of the class, with emphasis on the whole test. If there is any potential beneficiary of whom there is uncertainty, the trust will be void. Given Stamp LJ's interpretation of Lord Wilberforce's test, he could not agree with the majority that 'relatives' would be defined as 'descent from a common ancestor'. Instead, in holding 'relatives' was certain, he gave it the narrow definition of 'next of kin'.

Certainty of Objects: Certain concepts

2.22 Given the previous discussion, what will be certain concepts? Well, the concepts in McPhail v Doulton were all thought to be certain, even accepting the definitional difficulties posed by 'relatives'. So, directors, employees, etc, are certain; they are capable of objective definition. Problems arise with more subjective concepts, eg, 'friends'. Friends is subjective and differs from person to person: Do you know who your 'friends' are? As a class defining concept under a trust, 'friends' is (probably) an uncertain concept (obiter, per Browne-Wilkinson, J, in **Re Barlow (1979)**).

Certainty of Objects: Limits of the 'is/is not' test

2.23 First, the concept which defines the class must be clearly defined. Secondly, the discretionary trust may be void for what

Lord Wilberforce termed 'administrative unworkability'. Sometimes, the class could be so hopelessly wide that it would be impossible to administer the trust. For fear of prejudice to future cases, Lord Wilberforce hesitated to provide an example in McPhail, but did precisely that by stating that a trust for the residents of Greater London may be void for administrative unworkability. Perhaps influenced by this, a discretionary trust for the inhabitants of West Yorkshire was held to be void in **R v District Auditor, ex p West Yorkshire Metropolitan County Council (1986)**. Thirdly, a trust might also be void if the settlor is capricious.

What if a certainty is missing?

2.24 If one of the three certainties is missing, the trust is void. If the trust is void, what happens? It's too simplistic to state that the property will go back to the settlor; the answer to the question depends on which certainty is missing. If the trust is void for uncertainty of intention, the person who would have been the trustee takes the property as an outright gift (**Re Adams and the Kensington Vestry (1884)**). If the trust is void for uncertainty of subject-matter, it depends on whether it is void for (i) the property itself or (ii) the beneficial entitlement. If the property itself is uncertain, then the trust is simply void - no trust was created, so no property *technically* left the settlor (**Re London Wine (Shippers) Co Ltd (1986)**), but if the beneficial entitlement element of the subject-matter is void, then there is an automatic resulting trust of the beneficial interest to the estate (**Boyce v Boyce (1849)**). Finally, if the trust is void for uncertainty of objects, there is an automatic resulting trust of the beneficial interest back to the settlor, or their estate if the settlor is deceased (**Vandervell v IRC (1967)**).

Gifts Subject to a Condition Precedent

2.25 Normally, a gift will be made with no strings attached. Gifts subject to a condition precedent, on the other hand, impose a condition on the donee's enjoyment of the gift -

something which they have to satisfy before the gift can be made. Generally, anything might be attached as a condition precedent, so long as it isn't contrary to public policy. A good example comes from **Re Barlow (1979)**. This case concerned a legacy under a will whereby the testatrix permitted her 'friends' to purchase, at a discount, a painting from her house. The condition precedent was that the donee be the testatrix's friend. In this context, the term 'friends' was not offensive; this was a gift, not a trust. The term 'friends' was not being used to define a class of beneficiaries, rather as a condition for enjoyment. Therefore, Browne-Wilkinson J said that proof of friendship could be made to the executors of the estate by any 'reasonable test', suggesting that friendship is generally: (i) long-standing, (ii) social rather than business, (iii) and one where meetings are frequent.

CHAPTER 3
FORMALITIES AND
CONSTITUTION

Introduction

3.01 This chapter is concerned with the related topics of formalities and constitution. Though they are explained here under one chapter heading, they can be treated separately.

Formalities

3.02 When trusts lawyers speak of formalities, generally it specifically refers to **statutory formalities**. These are circumstances where Parliament has intervened to require that certain transactions require some form of writing. There are three key circumstances in which English trusts law requires some form of writing and these situations are the subject of this chapter. The first situation is where you wish to leave property on death and English law provides the 'will' for this purpose, setting out particular statutory requirements in order for a will to be valid. The second situation is where an individual wishes to declare a trust of land. Land, as you will know from your study of land law, generally requires formality of some kind. Finally, the third situation is where a beneficial owner wishes to dispose of their subsisting equitable interest. Each will now be taken in turn. All three situations share one thing in common: each requires some form of writing.

Wills

3.03 If you want to make specific provision of your property on death, then you should generally use a will. A valid will must comply with **s9, Wills Act 1837**. English law requires statutory formalities in relation to disposal of property on death because, evidently, in the event of a dispute, the one person who can provide the truth is dead. Section 9 Wills Act 1837 (amended by s17, Administration of Justice Act 1982) requires the following:

a) Writing (s9(a));

b) Signed by Testator (s9(a)) - the testator is the person making the will;

c) Testator intended by signature to give effect to the will (s9(b));

d) Signature is made or acknowledged by testator in the presence of two or more witnesses present at the time (s9(c));

e) Each witness attests and signs the will (s9(d)(i)) or acknowledges his signature in the presence of the testator (s9(d)(ii)).

3.04 Failure to comply with the requirements of the Wills Act renders the will void, and unless there is an earlier valid will, the testator will be deemed to have died intestate, ie, without a will. Even if a will appears to be valid, it may be challenged as failing to comply with s9, Wills Act 1837.

Section 53, Law of Property Act 1925

3.05 Students are warned that some statutory provisions in the law will be scary or cause them sleepless nights; section 53, Law of Property Act 1925 is such a scary provision. Well, only scary if you don't take the time to read this chapter. There are two key provisions: ss53(1)(b) and 53(1)(c). However, before considering both provisions, it is worth mentioning a third provision, namely s53(2). Section 53(2) is a potentially 'life-saving' provision; its effect is to suspend the formalities of s53 and can operate to save the unwitting claimant from defeat, if they can establish that a resulting, constructive, or implied trust was created on the facts. You'll see what this means below.

Trusts of Land – s53(1)(b), Law of Property Act 1925

3.06 Generally, the creation of an express trust in lifetime requires no formalities (**Paul v Constance (1977)**); the 'no formalities' requirement does not operate where the subject-matter of the express trust is land. Section 53(1)(b), Law of Property Act 1925 requires that a declaration of an express trust of land must be:

a) 'manifested and proved' (evidenced);

b) some writing;

c) signed by some person able to declare it. (Usually this is the settlor, though the language of the statute seems to leave the option open.)

3.07 Failure to comply with s53(1)(b) renders the declaration **unenforceable**, not void (**Gardner v Rowe (1828)**).

Relationship between s53(1)(b) and s53(2)

3.08 A good case which demonstrates the relationship between s53(1)(b) and s53(2) is **Hodgson v Marks (1971)**. Mrs Hodgson (H) took in lodgers at her house, one of whom was Mr Evans (E). H's nephew did not like E, whom he thought was up to no good. E persuaded H to convey the house into E's name, where it was orally agreed that H would be the beneficial owner. Naturally, the *oral* agreement did not comply with s53(1)(b) which requires signed, written, evidence of the trust, meaning that the declaration would be unenforceable. E then sold the house to Mr Marks (M), and E absconded with the purchase money, never to be seen again. That left H and M to fight over the house and whether M was bound by any interest H might have because of her occupation of the house – she was claiming a beneficial interest. The problem facing H was the oral agreement; s53(1)(b), because the subject-matter was land, requires signed, written, evidence of the trust, meaning that the declaration would be unenforceable without it. However, because there was a voluntary conveyance from H to E, there was a presumption of a resulting trust in H's favour which did not require formalities because of s53(2), LPA 1925. This meant that s53(2) operated to suspend the need to comply with s53(1)(b). Section 53(2) saved H, which meant that M was bound by her equitable interest which was protected by her actual occupation.

Disposition of Subsisting Equitable Interest – s53(1)(c), Law of Property Act 1925)

3.09 Section 53(1)(c) has a bit of a poor reputation among law students. It is a tricky provision, but the attempt made here is to de-mystify the provision so you never have to worry about it. One thing to make clear is that the following discussion relates to situations where the **trust already exists** and the **beneficiary is dealing with their equitable interest**. Remember, an equitable (beneficial) interest under a trust is property and the beneficiary can deal with it in much the same way as he would with other, tangible, property. So, the beneficiary might give it away, sell it, or declare a trust of it. The requirements of s53(1)(c), Law of Property Act 1925 are:

a) disposition of a **subsisting equitable interest**;

b) must be made **in writing**;

c) **signed** by transferor;

d) or their agent lawfully authorised in writing.

3.10 Note, the provision does not, unlike s53(1)(b), limit itself to land. Section 53(1)(c) applies to **all types of property**, and a failure to comply with the provision renders the purported disposition **void**.

3.11 We are now going to consider five scenarios which relate to dealings in the beneficial interest and in each scenario it is a matter of deciding whether s53(1)(c) applies to the proposed disposition. The five scenarios are: (i) Assignment of Equitable Interest; (ii) Instruction to Trustees to hold for Another; (iii) Sub-trust; (iv) Contract for Sale of Equitable Interest; (v) Miscellaneous (Nomination; Disclaimer).

(i) Assignment of Equitable Interest

3.12 This is undoubtedly the scenario with the most straightforward answer. Here, the beneficiary is seeking to transfer the equitable title to another so that the beneficiary retains no interest in it. Well, simply, this must be in writing and signed by the beneficiary or his lawfully authorised agent, otherwise the assignment is void.

(ii) Instruction to Trustee to hold for Another

3.13 This scenario is very similar to the first scenario, except that the beneficiary is involving the trustee in the transfer. In this scenario, the beneficiary instructs the trustee to hold the property for someone else. According to the House of Lords in **Grey v IRC (1960)**, this is a disposition of a subsisting equitable interest, so it must be in writing and signed in order to comply with s53(1)(c), Law of Property Act 1925. Additionally, their Lordships indicated that the word 'disposition' in the provision should have its ordinary meaning.

3.14 An interesting twist on the 'instruction to the trustee' scenario comes from the case of **Vandervell v IRC (1967)**. The Vandervell case is relatively simple. Let me tell you the story of Tony Vandervell. Vandervell (V) was a wealthy businessman. He dabbled in motor racing and enjoyed significant success with his motor racing team, 'Vanwall'. A serious accident to one of his drivers caused V to consider charitable uses for his wealth. V decided to endow a Chair of Pharmacology at the Royal College of Surgeons (RCS), but he went about it in an unusual way. I will break the actions into phases.

3.15 <u>Phase one</u>: V declared a bare trust of some shares in his engineering company. The trustee was his bank, and V was the beneficiary. V needed to transfer his equitable interest from himself to the RCS so the RCS would have funding (from dividends declared on the shares) to set up the Vandervell Chair of Pharmacology.

3.16 <u>Phase two</u>: V was advised that he should extract an option to re-purchase the shares from the RCS as a condition of the transfer.

3.17 <u>Phase three</u>: One day, V phoned his bank (the trustee) instructing it to transfer the shares to the RCS. This was an oral instruction, but was it sufficient to transfer of his interest?

3.18 The House of Lords held that because it was V's **intention that equitable title should pass** (so the RCS could have the benefit of share dividends), when V instructed the bank to transfer legal title in the shares to the RCS, the equitable title was taken by the legal title. This instruction was not one which was caught by s53(1)(c) and V's lack of writing did not mean the transfer was void. The *ratio decidendi* of the the case might be stated as follows: '**Where an absolutely entitled beneficiary instructs a trustee to transfer legal title to a third party *with the intention* that equitable title should also pass to the third party, then the legal title carries the equitable title. The instruction can be oral and section 53(1)(c) does not apply.**'

3.19 Importantly for Vandervell, his instruction and intention had the combined effect of moving both the legal and equitable title, whereas in **Grey v IRC**, the beneficiary was only moving the equitable title. Therefore, **Vandervell v IRC** fell outside s53(1)(c), Law of Property Act 1925, and became an exception to the provision. An important element of the decision in **Vandervell v IRC** was that Vandervell retained effective control over both the legal and equitable title under the bare trust in his favour. The Vandervell exception was confirmed by the case of **Soomro v Khuhawar (2015)**.

(iii) Sub-trust

3.20 The beneficiary can declare himself to be trustee to his own equitable interest for another; a sub-trust (a trust underneath the original trust). Does s53(1)(c) apply? The modern view is that it does not apply because it is essentially a new trust. In **Nelson v Greening and Sykes (Builders) Ltd (2008)**, the court indicated it would not be a disposition, so would not need to comply. This case appears to be supported by the more recent case of **Sheffield v Sheffield (2013)**. Such sub-trusts would need to comply with the three certainties, and if a sub-trust of land, also to comply with s53(1)(b), LPA 1925. Otherwise, there is no need to comply with s53(1)(c), LPA 1925.

3.21 The alternative, older view, is that a declaration of a sub-trust by the beneficiary in favour of another is a disposition – the old beneficiary is effectively removed from the trust (**Grainge v Wilberforce (1889)**). As such, the old beneficiary has disposed of a subsisting equitable interest, a transaction caught by s53(1)(c). If the declaration is not in writing and signed it will be void.

(iv) Contract for Sale of Equitable Interest;

3.22 Where the beneficiary sells his equitable interest, the question arises as to whether an oral contract is sufficient to effect the disposition, or whether such contracts have to be in writing to satisfy s53(1)(c). The answer seems to be whether the contract is specifically enforceable. Where a contract can attract the remedy of specific performance, before the contract is completed, a constructive trust arises in favour of the buyer. If a constructive trust arises, section 53(2) operates to suspend the formalities of s53(1)(c) (**Neville v Wilson (1997)**(CA)), applying Lord Radcliffe's dissent in **Oughtred v IRC (1960)**). Therefore, if the contract is for property which might attract the equitable remedy of specific performance, then s53(1)(c) might not need to be complied with. While each case must be taken on its particular facts, specific performance is generally awarded on contracts for the sale of land (which must, in any event, comply with s2, Law of Property (Miscellaneous Provisions) Act 1989), or for personal property which has a quality of uniqueness, or otherwise difficult to obtain from an alternative source, eg, shares in a private limited company.

(v) Miscellaneous (Nomination; Disclaimer).

3.23 This fifth category is quite obscure and unlikely to be something on which you would be assessed. It contains a mixed bag of situations which might engage the statutory formality under s53(1)(c), but probably do not. First, it is unlikely that a nomination under a pension fund is caught by s53(1)(c) (**Re Danish Bacon Co Staff Pension Fund Trusts (1971)**). Secondly, a disclaimer of an equitable interest may not engage s53(1)(c), or at least it did not in the case of **Re Paradise Motor Co Ltd (1968)**. Disclaimer is almost always likely to operate in an informal atmosphere, especially where the disclaimer is accompanied by swear words in the course of a family argument as in the Paradise Motor Co case.

Constitution

3.24 Once a trust has been validly declared, satisfying the three certainties, the trust **property must vest in the trustee**. If this does not occur, the trust is not constituted and will fail because 'equity will not assist a volunteer to perfect an imperfect gift' (**Milroy v Lord (1862)**). So, **constitution is simply the transfer of legal title from the transferor to the transferee**. If a gift, from the donor to the donee; if a trust, from the settlor to the trustee.

Conferring Benefit on Others

3.25 There are three methods of conferring a benefit on another: (1) **Gift**; (2) **Transfer on Trust**; (3) **Self-declaration of Trust**. In only situations (1) and (2) will the property need to be transferred to another, ie, constituted.

Situation (3) does not require constitution because the legal title is already with the trustee. The courts will not interpret a failed gift as a self-declaration of trust (**Milroy v Lord (1862)**).

Different Types of Property

3.26 The method used to transfer property will depend on the type of property in question. The most common forms of property and their methods of transfer are listed in this table:

PROPERTY TYPE	METHOD
Land	Legal title to land should pass by deed (**s52, Law of Property Act 1925**); a 'deed' is defined in **s1, Law of Property (Miscellaneous Provisions) Act 1989** as a document which is signed, witnessed, delivered, and indicates on its face that it is a 'deed'.
Chattels (Personal Property)	There is a formal way and an informal way to transfer legal title to a chattel. The formal way involves executing a deed of gift which must comply with the requirements for a **deed**. This would not occur in respect of most gifts of personal property. The most common way is by immediate intention to give and delivery of the item (**Re Cole (1963)**). Note, it is the

	intention to give which must be immediate, not the delivery of the item.
Bank account	As a property type, a bank account is a 'chose in action'; intangible property. It is a debt. If your account is in credit, it is a debt which the bank owes you; if overdrawn, it is a debt you owe to the bank (**Foley v Hill (1848)**). Legal title to a 'chose in action' passes by complying with **s136, Law of Property Act 1925**. This requires that signed, written notice of the transfer be given to the debtor, ie, the bank.
Copyright	By **s90(3), Copyright, Designs, and Patents Act 1988** the assignment of copyright must be in writing and signed by or on behalf of the assignor.
Shares	Where the shares are traded outside the CREST system, legal title is transferred by executing a stock transfer form (**s1, Stock Transfer Act 1963**) and sending it, with the old share certificate, to the company for registration. The old share certificate will be cancelled and a new one issued.

3.27 Where the property in question is transferred correctly, the trust is completely constituted or the gift is complete. There is nothing more to be done for the transfer to take effect. Where the transfer is incomplete, then equity will not assist a volunteer to perfect an imperfect gift (or trust) (**Milroy v Lord (1852)**). However, this is not strictly the case since there are instances where equity has intervened to assist the volunteer. There are four well-established exceptions, and a fifth which is more controversial: (1) **The Donatio Mortis Causa**; (2) **The rule in Strong v Bird**; (3) **Proprietary Estoppel**; (4) **The rule in Re Rose**; and, (5) **Choithram and Pennington**.

(1) Exception: The Donatio Mortis Causa (Death-bed gift)

3.28 Gifts made by the donor on his death-bed have been a well-established exception to the maxim that equity will not assist a volunteer to perfect an imperfect gift. If a donor lies at point of death, English law allows an informally made gift to be valid so long as three conditions are satisfied:

(i) Gift made in contemplation of imminent death;

3.29 The donor is required to contemplate his end as imminent, or impending. This is not contemplation of death as a possibility, but something which the donor appreciates from the circumstances. For example, the donor might be in his hospital bed where he is receiving treatment for a condition which the medical experts said has a poor prognosis. If he were to attempt a gift in this context, it may well be that he is deemed to be contemplating his death as imminent. A good example of contemplating death as imminent, and contemplating death as a possibility, comes from the case of **Re Miller (1961)** where the donor was about to take a flight and had a fear of air travel. She attempted to make a gift of a life insurance policy to her sister in the event of her death. Well, the donor did die when the plane collided with an Italian fighter jet over Anzio, and the issue of whether a valid DMC might make the gift valid arose. Although the report is a poor one, it is clear that death should not be contemplated as a possibility, but as something which is imminent or impending. This was re-iterated by the recent case of **King v Chiltern Dog Rescue (2015)**.

(ii) Gift is conditional on death;

3.30 The idea behind this condition is that if the donor should make a recovery, the gift is automatically revoked. In many cases, the courts will be willing to presume that death-bed gifts are revoked by the survival of the donor. Of course, it will also be satisfied by express wording such as, 'if I die'. However, in most cases the conditionality of the gift is presumed.

(iii) Actual or constructive delivery of the gift.

3.31 The donor must part with dominium (or control) of the property in question. This will most easily be satisfied in the case of small chattels, eg, jewellery, an expensive watch, etc. But what happens when the donor wishes to give a car, or land? Well, this is where constructive delivery is allowed. In the case of a car, constructive delivery occurs by delivery of the keys, even if it is unclear whether other sets of keys exist (**Woodward v Woodward (1992)**). In the case of **Sen v Headley (1991)**, the key to a box containing deeds to a house was sufficient to be constructive delivery of the land. Although, it may have been crucial in the case that title to the land in question was unregistered. Whether this would work where title is registered is unclear.

(2) Exception: The rule in Strong v Bird

3.32 This is a very narrow exception and one of, in some instances, pure fluke. This is perhaps why this is sometimes known as the 'rule of fortuitous vesting'. The rule in **Strong v Bird (1874)** operates where the donee of an incomplete lifetime gift becomes the executor of the donor's estate on the donor's death. The 'accident' of the donee becoming the donor's executor vests title to the property in the donee (as executor) and thereby perfects the gift.

3.33 Let me explain it with an example: Bob wants to give Colin his antique vase. To make a lifetime gift of the antique vase, Bob must (i) have an immediate intention to make a gift and (ii) deliver the property to Colin. Now, let us assume that there is clear immediate intention to give the antique vase, but Bob is delayed in delivering the item and Bob dies the next day. On normal principles, the gift failed in lifetime because although the intention was immediate, no delivery was made so the gift fails. Unlucky, Colin. However, when Bob's will is opened, it is discovered that Colin is to be executor of the estate. Therefore, the gift could be completed by this 'accident' and Colin may receive the antique vase, provided the other conditions are satisfied.

3.34 The conditions for the rule in Strong v Bird to operate are:

> (i) There must be an immediate intention to make the gift (**Re Freeland(1952)**);
>
> (ii) Intention continues until the death of the donor (**Re Gonin (1979)**);
>
> (iii) Donee is appointed as executor of the donor's estate.

3.35 The case of Strong v Bird itself concerned the discharge of a debt, where the executor was the debtor and the testator the creditor. It was held that the debtor's appointment as executor of the creditor's estate discharged the debt. That is a principle of extremely narrow application so the case was extended to apply to gifts by the case of **Re Stewart (1908)**. The rule also applies where the donee becomes administrator of the estate of an intestate donor (**Re James (1935)**). Of more controversy is whether the rule applies to perfect a trust where the trustee of a failed lifetime trust is appointed executor of the deceased settlor's estate. The case which is often cited as authority for the proposition that the rule should apply to perfect an imperfect trust as well as an imperfect gift is **Re Ralli (1964)**. This case is not the strongest authority on the point, but it is the best we have that might be said to extend the rule to perfect an imperfect trust. However, it is controversial in that it might well be said that the roles of executor and trustee are entirely different.

(3) Exception: Proprietary Estoppel

3.36 Equitable Estoppel is a well-established principle of English law. Proprietary estoppel is capable of conferring rights on a claimant where an assurance is given that the claimant will receive an interest in property. However, that alone is insufficient since the claimant must then rely on the assurance to their detriment (**Gillett v Holt (2001)(CA)**; **Thorner v Major (2009)(HL)**). If the claimant is able to satisfy these elements, it gives rise to an inchoate equity – an incomplete equity. The equity is made complete by a remedy which is discretionary and the remedy is the minimum necessary to do justice. It is worth noting that establishing the equity may not result in the claimant receiving what they were promised.

(4) Exception: The rule in Re Rose

3.37 Confusingly, there are two cases by the name of **Re Rose** on a very similar point: one in 1949, the other in 1952. Both cases concerned a gift of shares in a private company. In both cases, the donor had completed the necessary documentation and sent it to the company for registration of the donee as the new owner. However, in neither case was the transfer complete by the death of the donor, which became important for tax assessment purposes. In both cases the court held that since the donor had done everything necessary to transfer title, the transfer was effective in equity, with the registration of the donee as the legal owner a formality to be completed later. These cases can be contrasted with **Re Fry (1946)** where the donor had not done everything necessary to transfer title to shares because he had not obtained HM Treasury consent beforehand, so the gift in Re Fry failed. Therefore, the rule in Re Rose is a simple idea. So long as the donor/settlor has done all they can to transfer title to the property in question, but waits on the actions of a third party, eg, a company registrar, then the gift/trust will be complete in equity.

3.38 In **Mascall v Mascall (1985)**, a father made a gift of a house to his son. The father completed all the necessary documentation to transfer the property and handed it to his son, but before delivery to the Land Registry, they fell out after an argument. The father sought to revoke the gift, but the CA held that, applying Re Rose, the father had done all within his power to transfer title. Therefore, this operated as a slight gloss on **Re Rose** where the transfer will be regarded as complete in equity where the necessary documentation has been handed to the donee.

3.39 An interesting recent case is **Collins v Simonsen (2019)**, which concerned the transfer of £42,000 from the transferor to an estate agent for the purpose of paying rent on a flat which was going to be rented by the transferee; effectively, the transferor was going to pay the transferee's rent. However, the money was transferred without instruction to the estate agent and, in those circumstances, it was held on resulting trust for the transferor. The transferor had not done everything in her power to perfect the gift, which she could have done by indicating to the estate agent the purpose of the transfer of funds.

(5) Exception: Choithram and Pennington

3.40 The most significant recent cases are **T Choithram International SA v Pagarani (2001)** and **Pennington v Waine (2002)**.

3.41 In **T Choithram International SA v Pagarani (2001)** the Privy Council had to determine the legality of a novel situation. The settlor wanted to create a charitable trust so he declared a trust with nine trustees, one of whom was the settlor himself – a crucial fact as it turned out. However, what the settlor failed to do was transfer legal title to the trust property to all nine trustees, so that at his death the trust property was vested solely in the settlor, that is, it had not been constituted. Prior to his death, the settlor called a number of people to his bed and stated 'I give my property to the trust' (or words very similar). Naturally, given that the property at issue was shares and deposits in a bank account, this statement was not enough to transfer legal title to that property to all the trustees. Nevertheless, the PC took account of the words in the context used and said that words of gift, in this context, could only mean a gift to the trustees of the foundation. They were not words of outright gift, but words of 'gift on trust'. Thus, **where one out of a larger body of trustees has the trust property vested solely in him, words of gift to the trust are to be interpreted as words of gift on trust to the trustees of the foundation**. After death, the executor of the settlor's estate can be compelled to transfer formally to all trustees. This is a generous interpretation of the language to make the declaration valid.

3.42 The case of **T Choithram International SA v Pagarani** marked a shift in judicial approach to constitution, indicating a more liberal approach, something which was subsequently embraced by the Court of Appeal in **Pennington v Waine (2002)**.

3.43 The case of **Pennington v Waine** concerned a gift of shares from an aunt (donor) to a nephew (donee). The donor completed the stock transfer form, but did not send it to the company for registration. Instead, she handed it to her agent. Additionally, she informed the donee of the gift, he became a director of the company (a requirement of the company's articles of association), and the agent assured the donee that everything would be completed. Regrettably, for the donee, the transfer was incomplete on the donor's death, meaning the shares would form part of the donor's estate. The donee, as a volunteer, had to demonstrate an exception operated to save the gift. The rule in Re Rose didn't operate because the donor had not done everything within her power; the donee wasn't executor, so the rule in Strong v Bird couldn't apply, nor was the gift made on the donor's death-bed. Unfazed by these difficulties, the CA held that the gift of shares was valid. The court relied on the notion of 'unconscionability'. Conscience was the foundation stone of equity and it was resurrected in this case. Arden LJ suggested that even where Re Rose was not met, a point might arise in the case where it would be unconscionable for the donor to deny the gift. The material facts in Pennington v Waine might be listed as:

(1) The gift was made voluntarily;

(2) The donor informed the donee of the gift;

(3) The donor completed the stock transfer documents;

(4) The donee became a director of the company (a requirement of the articles of association), suffering a detriment;

(5) The donor handed the documentation to her agent (the company's auditor) who informed the donee there was nothing more to be done.

3.44 All these factors taken together were sufficient to make it unconscionable to deny the gift. As a postscript, the donee didn't actually receive the shares since a separate case concerning the same shares determined that the gift by the donor was made in breach of a right of pre-emption which should have been given to the existing shareholders; all that effort, ultimately, for nothing.

3.45 The judicial reception to the case of Pennington was somewhat lukewarm and it seems to have largely been confined to its special facts by **Zeital v Kaye (2010)**. See, also, **Curtis v Pulbrook (2011)** for similarly muted reaction.

CHAPTER 4
SECRET TRUSTS

Introduction

4.01 Sometimes, there are things which people want to keep quiet. In life, of course, this can be achieved, but on death, valid dispositions of property must comply with the section 9, Wills Act 1837 (chapter three). Any trust set up under a will, or any gift of property under a will, must comply with these provisions and be stated on the face of the will. A will is a public document and, as such, any gifts or trusts set up in your will are available for all the world to see after your death. However, secret trusts allow the testator to keep the beneficiary out of the will; they keep the trust or the beneficiary, a secret. There are two forms of secret trust: the **fully secret trust** (FST), and the **half secret trust** (HST). Broadly, secret trusts, whether fully or half secret, are created in a similar manner, with one crucial difference.

Fully Secret Trusts (FST)

4.02 A FST is one which looks on the face of the will like an outright gift to the person who would be the secret trustee. Nothing about the trust is revealed; it's fully secret. The requirements for a fully secret trust were summarised in **Ottaway v Norman (1971)** by Brightman J:

(i) Intention on the part of the testator;

4.03 The testator must intend to create a trust: certainty of intention. If the intention is unclear, then the secret trustee takes the property outright.

(ii) Communication of that intention to the secret trustee;

4.04 Communication may be made by the testator himself, or by the testator's agent, but it must be prior to the testator's death. If the secret is discovered in the testator's papers after death, the trust is unenforceable and the secret trustee takes the property absolutely, ie, free of the secret trust. The testator must communicate the terms of the secret trust in full or, sometimes, communication may take place by placing instructions in a sealed envelope marked – 'Not to be opened until after my death'. Provided the secret trustee understands that the document contains the terms of a trust, that will suffice (**Re Keen (1937)**). Lord Wright MR in Re Keen drew an analogy with a ship sailing under sealed orders.

(iii) Acceptance by the secret trustee;

4.05 This can be made expressly or impliedly (**Wallgrave v Tebbs (1855)**), and may be satisfied even by the silence of the secret trustee (**Moss v Cooper (1861)**).

(iv) Reliance by the testator.

4.06 The testator must rely on the secret trustee's acceptance. Reliance can be achieved in three ways: (a) the testator will make a will in terms consistent with the communication; or, (b) leave an existing will unchanged (remember, communication can occur after the will is executed for a FST); or, (c) not make a will at all and allow the rules of intestacy to take the property to the secret trustee. Naturally, for option (c), the secret trustee will have to be entitled to your estate on your death under the Administration of Estates Act 1925.

Half Secret Trusts (HST)

4.07 A HST is different from a FST in that the trust is mentioned in the will, but the beneficiary is not. A good example would be: '£100,000 to Eric, on terms which I have already communicated to him.' Here, anyone reading the will would see there is a trust, but have no knowledge of the beneficiary; it's half secret. Broadly, the requirements for HSTs are the same as those for FSTs, save for one crucial difference – Communication and acceptance of a HST must take place before the execution of the will (**Blackwell v Blackwell (1927)**). Of course, this timing difference impacts the reliance issue. In reliance on the acceptance, the testator must then make the will, or not make a will, in the latter case allowing intestacy to give the secret trustee the property.

The key debates in secret trusts

-Does s53(1)(b), LPA 1925 apply to secret trusts of land?

4.08 A declaration of a trust of land must be evidenced by signed writing (**s53(1)(b), LPA 1925**). Whether the provision applies to secret trusts is unclear as there is conflicting authority. In **Re Baillie (1886)**, a HST of land was invalid for lack of signed, written, evidence to comply with s53(1)(b). However, the decision is weakened since it was decided before HSTs were recognised in English law – this did not happen until the House of Lords decision in **Blackwell v Blackwell (1929)**. In **Ottaway v Norman (1971)**, a FST of land was valid without signed, written, evidence to comply with the provision, but Brightman J did not discuss s53(1)(b), LPA 1925, so the decision might be seen as *per incuriam*, ie, taken without consideration of relevant law. Therefore, this question remains without a conclusive answer, but the answer might lie in whether one regards secret trusts as express trusts or constructive trusts. If the former, the provision should probably be applied, but if the latter, then s53(2), LPA 1925 removes the need to comply with the formalities of s53(1)(b), LPA 1925.

4.09 In **Kasperbauer v Griffiths (2000)**, the court was willing to regard secret trusts as constructive trusts meaning that the formalities of s53(1)(b), LPA 1925 would not operate because of s53(2), LPA 1925. However, this statement was merely obiter.

-Can a secret trustee disclaim a legacy?

4.10 Under normal circumstances, if the beneficiary does not want a legacy which they have been given under a will, they can disclaim it, ie, give it up. However, the matter is not as straightforward with secret trusts since the beneficiary is not giving up their interest, their disclaimer is defeating the secret beneficiary. In **Re Maddock (1902)(CA)**, in the context of a FST, it was said that disclaimer by secret trustee would defeat the trust because the personal obligation imposed on the trustee would disappear by disclaiming. In contrast, in **Blackwell v Blackwell (1927)(HL)**, it was said that the court would intervene to prevent a secret trust from failing. This would be an application of the equitable maxim – **equity will not allow a trust to fail for want of a trustee**. In terms of a conclusive position, neither Maddock nor Blackwell can be said to provide that since, in both cases, the comments were obiter dicta.

-Can a beneficiary signatory to a will still benefit notwithstanding s15, WA 1837?

4.11 Section 15, Wills Act 1837 provides that a witness to a will forfeits any gift they might have been allocated under the will. However, in the case of **Re Young (1951)**, the secret beneficiary was a signatory to the will, but this did not defeat his interest. Danckwerts J said that the secret trust did not operate under the will, rather that it took effect outside the will by the communication and acceptance of the trust during the testator's lifetime.

-Communication to joint tenants?

4.12 The testator should communicate the terms of the trust to all intended trustees. If this does not occur, only the trustees who are informed of the trust are bound. An exception to this is where the secret trustees are joint tenants and communication is made to at least one of them before the will is executed (**Re Stead (1900)**). A joint tenancy occurs where there are multiple owners of property. An example of a joint tenancy would be: '£100,000 to Alison and Barney.' Here, Alison and Barney are joint tenants of the £100,000 because there are no words of severance. Words of severance give the parties a defined interest in the property and create a tenancy in common. So, a tenancy in common would be: '£100,000 to Alison and Barney *equally*.' In this situation, the word, 'equally' operates to sever the property giving each a defined interest. Only in the first example would the rule in Re Stead apply.

-Pre-decease?

4.13 Central to all trusts is the issue of constitution. When does constitution take place in a secret trust, ie, when does the secret trustee get the legal title? The answer is that the secret trustee gets legal title when the will or intestacy rules allow it, ie, some time after the death of the testator. That is a position which anyone would understand, but secret trusts are complicated by this odd case of **Re Gardner (No 2)(1923)**. In this case, the secret beneficiary pre-deceased the testator. Normally, the gift would lapse and stay with the estate, but in this case the court held that the beneficial interest passed to the estate of the secret beneficiary. The judge held that since the secret trust arose outside the will by communication and acceptance, the interest had arisen before the secret beneficiary's death. The decision is not without its problems. First, the interest arises before the trust is constituted; this is contrary to principle. Secondly, if the interest arises, then a property right is created in favour of the secret beneficiary meaning any attempt by the testator to change his will or change his mind would be an interference with the secret beneficiary's property rights; again, this is contrary to principle because a will is a revocable document in English law. Whether Re Gardner (No 2) will be followed in the future is questionable, but it remains good law.

Rationale for Secret Trusts

4.14 Given the clash between the Wills Act 1837 and the secret trust, justifying secret trusts is important. There are two theories often put forward to justify secret trusts: the **'fraud theory'** and the **'dehors the will theory'** ('outside the will theory). The fraud theory is that which is traditionally put forward to justify enforcing secret trusts. It would be a fraud on the testator if the secret trust were denied (**Moss v Cooper (1869)**), and also on the secret beneficiary (Hodge [1980] Conv 341). The maxim is that 'equity will not allow a statute (Wills Act 1837) to be used as an instrument of fraud'. However, the fraud argument only really works for FSTs, since HSTs make it clear on the face of the will that a trust is intended, so there is no question of defrauding the testator. Therefore, we look for an alternative justification for enforcing secret trusts and it comes in the form of the 'dehors the will' theory. The 'dehors the will' theory, sometimes referred to as the 'outside the will' theory, is the idea that secret trusts are not, technically, testamentary dispositions and, therefore, there is no conflict with any provisions in the Wills Act 1837 (**Blackwell v Blackwell (1929)**) because they do not need to comply with it. The secret trust arises once communication and acceptance of the terms of the secret trust occur in lifetime; the only function of the will is to constitute the trust, ie, to transfer legal title to the property to the secret trustee. The 'dehors the will theory' was used to justify the decisions in the cases of **Re Young (1951)** and **Re Gardner (No 2)(1923)**.

What type of trust are secret trusts?

4.15 Closely linked to the rationale for secret trusts is the question over whether secret trusts are express trusts or constructive trusts. Express trusts are those which are expressly created giving effect to the intention of the settlor; constructive trusts are imposed by law, typically to prevent fraud. Naturally, therefore, if one adheres to the 'fraud theory' for justifying secret trusts, then it is more reasonable to regard secret trusts as constructive. However, if secret trusts operate outside the will, by the communication and acceptance of the terms of the secret trust to the secret trustee, then they are better regarded as express.

Modern Uses for Secret Trusts

4.16 Recently, the secret trust concept has been utilised outside the wills context. In **Gold v Hill (1999)**, an individual made a lifetime nomination of his solicitor as beneficiary under a life insurance policy, giving the solicitor a separate instruction as to the true beneficiary. This was upheld by the court. In the case of **Kasperbauer v Griffith (1997)**, the secret trust was purportedly used as part of a tax avoidance strategy. Although it failed, the case does raise the prospect of using secret trusts for tax avoidance.

Postscript

4.17 One final point should be noted about secret trusts. The Money Laundering, Terrorist Financing and Transfer of Funds (Information on the Payer) Regulations 2017, SI 2017/692 impose an obligation to maintain a public register of beneficial ownership as a mechanism to counter money laundering. Part of the obligation involves identification of the beneficiary. Naturally, if this is as it seems, it will have a dramatic impact on the secret trust and its future.

CHAPTER 5
PRIVATE PURPOSE TRUSTS

Introduction

5.01 Trusts should be for people not purposes, unless those purposes are charitable. Therefore, generally, the beneficiary should be human. However, there are a number of anomalous purpose trusts which do not have a human beneficiary and which are not for a public purpose. These are anomalies, but enforceable in English law.

The 'beneficiary principle'

5.02 In **Morice v Bishop of Durham (1804)** it was stated that there must be somebody in whose favour the court can enforce the trust, and that person should be human, otherwise the trust is void. Only a human can determine whether a trust is being carried out; only a human can complain to the courts. This is the 'beneficiary principle'. The 'beneficiary principle' is closely linked to the concept of certainty of objects; the objects of a trust must be certain, and they must be human. However, law would not be law without exceptions, and there are a number of exceptions to the 'beneficiary principle'. These are not charitable trusts, but said to be valid as non-charitable purposes trusts. They are sometimes referred to as trusts of imperfect obligations; they are valid, but unenforceable – there is no human to enforce them if the trustee does not carry them out. One final point before considering the exceptions: charitable trusts, though trusts for purposes, are enforced by the Attorney-General and regulated, in most cases, by the Charity Commission.

Exceptions to the 'beneficiary principle'

5.03 The exceptions to the 'beneficiary principle' are trusts for the maintenance of particular animals, for the saying of private masses, and for the erection and maintenance of monuments and graves. These were described by Underhill as concessions to human weakness, and as a category they are, technically, closed (**Re Endacott (1960)**). However, recent developments in the case of **Re Denley (1969)**, suggest there may be life in private purposes.

(a) Animals;

5.04 A testator may, in his will, leave funds on trust for the maintenance of their animals. Note, the trust has to be for the individual animal, not for animals generally. A trust for animals generally would be a charitable trust (**Re Wedgewood (1915)**).

5.05 There are several cases where funds have been left for the maintenance of particular or individual animals. In **Pettingall v Pettingall (1842)** money was left to care for the testator's horse, and in **Re Dean (1889)**, for the testator's horses and hounds.

(b) Masses;

5.06 A testator may leave funds for the saying of a private mass for his departed soul (**Bourne v Keane (1919)(HL)**). If the mass is public, then it is charitable (**Re Hetherington (1990)**).

(c) Monuments;

5.07 A testator may leave funds for the erection or maintenance of a monument or tomb (**Mussett v Bingle (1876)**; **Re Hooper (1932)**). Funds left for the maintenance of the entire church or graveyard would be charitable (**Re Douglas (1905)**). Alternatively, a person may contract with the local authority for the local authority to maintain a grave, or memorial for a period of not more than 99 years (**s1, The Parish Councils and Burial Authorities (Misc**

Provisions) Act 1970). The erection of a monument may be charitable where it can be shown to be for a public benefit. In **Earl Mountbatten of Burma Statue Appeal Trust (1981)**, the Charity Commission upheld as charitable a statue to the memory of Earl Mountbatten as it was likely to inspire noble and heroic deeds.

(d) Re Denley style trust.

5.08 The three anomalous exceptions to the 'beneficiary principle' were well-established, if not universally loved, when a case which challenged the conventions on private purpose trusts arose: **Re Denley's Trust Deed (1969)**. In this case, land was given to trustees to be held on trust for the purpose of providing a recreation or sports ground for the employees of a company and some others. This was not strictly a trust for people because of the stated purpose, but as a purpose trust it didn't fit into the established categories and, therefore, should have been void. Nevertheless, the trust was upheld as valid, and none of the difficulties seemed to bother Goff J.

5.09 This trust, though it was expressed as a purpose, actually benefited **identifiable individuals** who could enforce the trust by injunction (if necessary). Note, Goff J didn't refer to the individuals as beneficiaries; he was careful to avoid that label. The case was applied subsequently in **Re Lipinski's Will Trusts (1976)**.

5.10 Two final points about Re Denley should be made. First, the trust had a perpetuity period. In other words, the length of time the trust could last was limited by the trust deed. Secondly, at the end of the trust, the property was to pass outright to a named charity.

Perpetuity rules

5.11 No trust, unless charitable, can last forever. Private purpose trusts will come to an end at some point. In law, they are brought to an end by the perpetuity rules. Now, the perpetuity rules are complex, but the one which applies to private purpose trusts is simple. This is the rule of excessive duration (or, the rule against inalienability). This rule effectively states that if you want to erect and maintain a tomb, or maintain an animal, or say a mass, you cannot do it forever; English law will draw the trust to a close.

5.12 The rule against excessive duration is rather quaint and all trusts will be limited to a **human life in being plus 21 years**. Thus, if I leave £10,000 to maintain my pet dog, Oscar, after my death and that the trust should last for the life of my sister, Charlotte, then 21 years, the trust will last as long as Charlotte lives, then when she dies, the clock starts to tick down for a further 21 years when, eventually, the trust will come to an end. Obviously, for most domestic pets, 21 years will be enough, but the perpetuity period should still be stated.

5.13 However, there are some quirks to the perpetuity rules, and though a perpetuity period for a private purpose trust should generally be a human life in being and 21 years, or a nominated fixed period of not more than 21 years, some cases have rather curious value.

5.14 In **Re Hooper (1932)**, a clause for as long as the law allows was upheld, it being interpreted as 21 years. This applied **Pirbright v Salwey (1896)**, where similar language was used.

5.15 In **Mussett v Bingle (1876)**, no perpetuity clause was nominated either for the erection or the maintenance of the monument. The court was willing to assume that the £300 set aside for the erection of the monument would be used to build the monument within 21 years, but that the £200 set aside to maintain the monument was void for perpetuity.

5.16 The lives of animals cannot be used as the measure (**Re Kelly (1932)**), and in **Re Dean (1889)**, the court allowed a perpetuity period which was fixed at 50 years. The case is undoubtedly wrong on this point, but not yet overruled.

5.17 The Perpetuities and Accumulations Act 1964 does not apply to private purpose trusts (s15(4)); likewise the Perpetuities and Accumulations Act 2009 (s18).

The Quistclose Trust

5.18 The Quistclose trust takes its name from the House of Lords decision of **Barclays Bank Ltd v Quistclose Investments Ltd (1970)**. Quistclose trusts tend to involve the payment of money from one party to another which is for a particular purpose and not at the free disposal of the recipient.

Creation

5.19 Following a flurry of recent cases, what is required to create a Quistclose Trust is relatively well-settled. In **Bieber v Teathers (2012)** at first instance, and confirmed on appeal, it was stated that what is required is that the funds transferred are **not at the free disposal of the recipient**. This is to be determined by looking at the terms of the arrangement or to objectively ascertain them from the circumstances of the transaction. What is central is the mutual intention of payer and recipient **objectively** determined; their subjective opinion is not relevant.

5.20 Though it is not a requirement that the funds are segregated in a separate account (**Twinsectra v Yardley (2002)**), where the funds are segregated it can provide valuable evidence that a Quistclose trust was intended.

5.21 It is the case that intention is crucial; not the form in which the Quistclose was created. Thus, an agreement made orally will be sufficient, but there are difficulties of proof.

5.22 If the requirements are met, then an equitable obligation arises which will be enforced by the courts on the basis that it is unconscionable for the recipient of funds to retain them knowing that there is an obligation attached to the receipt.

5.23 To these, the CA in **Bieber v Teathers (2012)**, added that it was it was crucial to pay close regard to the circumstances of the transfer and any contractual documentation between the parties. The crucial thing is that the search is on for a **clear intention that the money is not to become the absolute property of the recipient**.

Juridical Basis

5.24 One of the controversies in relation to the Quistclose trust is what is the legal (juridical) basis of the Quistclose trust: what sort of trust is it?

5.25 In **Barclay's Bank Ltd v Quistclose Investments Ltd (1970)**, Lord Wilberforce said that there were two trusts; a primary trust for the purpose identified and if the primary trust fails, a secondary trust in favour of the payer. His Lordship is careful not to label either of these trusts, but the suggestion would seem to be that the primary trust might be express and the secondary trust a resulting trust.

5.26 The most comprehensive review of the legal basis for the Quistclose trust was given by Lord Millett in **Twinsectra v Yardley (2002)** where his Lordship concluded that it was an orthodox example of a resulting trust.

5.27 This is a limited flavour of the law. If you would like a more extensive understanding of the competing views of the Quistclose trust, the leading work is Swadling (ed), The Quistclose Trust: Critical Essays (Hart Publishing, 2004).

CHAPTER 6
CHARITABLE TRUSTS

Introduction

6.01 Over the last 15 years, the law on charities has undergone a significant amount of reform and consolidation. In this chapter, we consider what conditions an organisation must satisfy in order to obtain charitable status.

6.02 The modern law of charities is found in the Charities Act 2011 ('CA 2011') and case law. The organisation with responsibility for regulation and oversight of the charitable sector is the Charity Commission.

Benefits of charitable status

6.03 There are many benefits of charitable status. The most obvious benefit is that charities enjoy significant **tax exemptions**, but charities are also **exempt from the perpetuity rules**, meaning that charities could *potentially* go on forever.

Definition of a charity

6.04 In England and Wales, a charity is an **organisation** established **solely for charitable purposes** and is **subject to the jurisdiction of the High Court** over charities (**s1(1)**, **CA 2011**).

6.05 Section 2, CA 2011 defines a charitable purposes as one which is listed in **s3, CA 2011** and which is for the **public benefit**.

Charitable Purposes

6.06 The charitable purposes are:

>   - the prevention or relief of poverty;
>
>   - the advancement of education;
>
>   - the advancement of religion;
>
>   - the advancement of health or the saving of lives;
>
>   - the advancement of the arts, culture, heritage or science;
>
>   - the advancement of amateur sport;
>
>   - the advancement of human rights, conflict resolution or reconciliation, or the promotion of religious or racial harmony or equality and diversity;
>
>   - the advancement of environmental protection or improvement;
>
>   - the relief of those in need, by reason of youth, age, ill-health, disability, financial hardship or other disadvantage;
>
>   - the advancement of animal welfare;
>
>   - the promotion of the efficiency of the armed forces of the Crown or of the police, fire and rescue services or ambulance services;
>
>   - any other purposes currently recognised as charitable and any new charitable purposes which are similar to another charitable purpose.

6.07 Many of these charitable purposes were in existence prior to the CA 2011, but the key point is that they have been individually identified. The prevention of poverty is a new charitable head, whereas the relief of poverty was always a charitable object. Though this in itself was quite a radical change, the advancement of amateur sport was arguably more radical. This is because charitable trusts promoting amateur sports always had to be linked to education in order to be valid.

6.08 Those aside, perhaps the most radical of the charitable heads is the advancement of human rights, etc., since this is sometimes viewed as political activity, which is something forbidden under charities law. That said, promoting human rights and the wider understanding of human rights is broadly neutral in its approach and unlikely to be political.

6.09 Charitable trusts must be **wholly and exclusively charitable** and if there are other non-charitable purposes which operate under the umbrella of the charity, then the charitable trust will be void unless those non-charitable purposes are merely incidental (**Re Coxen (1948)**).

Public Benefit

6.10 As well as falling within one of the charitable heads, a charitable trust must also manifest a clear **public benefit** (**s2(1)(b)**, **CA 2011**). All charities must demonstrate a public benefit. The former presumption of public benefit in relation to some charitable purposes no longer operates.

6.11 The Charity Commission has issued **guidance** on dealing with the question of whether a charity satisfies the public benefit (**ss14(2)** and **17(1)**, **CA 2011**).

6.12 There are two key principles to the public benefit: first, **there must be an identifiable benefit or benefits** and, secondly, **the benefit must be to the public or a section of the public**. These two principles are sub-divided for purposes of providing detail and clarification.

6.13 Where there is an identifiable benefit or benefits, **it must be clear what the benefits are** and that the **benefits are related to the aims**. The third element is that any **benefits must be balanced against any harm**. A good case on this point is **National Anti-Vivisection Society v IRC (1948)**) where the benefits of animal testing to human health outweighed any moral benefits which might arise from the abolition of animal testing.

6.14 The second principle, that **the benefit must be to the public or a section of the public** is also sub-divided into categories. First, the **beneficiaries must be appropriate to the aims** and, secondly, **where the benefit is restricted to a section of the public, the opportunity to benefit must not be unreasonably restricted**. This means that where the charity is not for the public at large, any restriction will be valid if reasonable, eg, a public space for recreation in a particular town might be for the benefit of inhabitants of that town.

6.15 Thirdly, **those in poverty should not be excluded**. This can pose difficulties where charities charge for entrance or for their services. However, it is possible to deal with the issue by offering discounts to those on lower incomes.

6.16 Fourthly, and finally, **private benefits must be incidental**. A charitable trust should pursue wholly and exclusively charitable purposes, but if there is an incidental private benefit this will not invalidate the trust as, for example, in **Re Coxen (1948)** where the trust deed provided that a dinner be provided for the trustees every year.

Political Activities

6.17 A charitable trust cannot pursue political purposes, nor can its funds be used to support a political party or a particular election candidate, However, revised Charity Commission guidance does allow for political campaigning as long as it is linked to the charity's purposes.

6.18 However, if charities wish to pursue clearly political purposes then this may be achieved by undertaking such activity through a separate organisation. This was the position of Amnesty International which undertook its charitable activities through its principal charitable arm, whereas its political activity was undertaken in the name of a private company,

The cy-près doctrine

6.19 When a private trust fails, there is an automatic resulting trust of the beneficial interest for the settlor. However, where a charitable trust fails, the **cy-près doctrine may operate** to allow the funds to be diverted to a similar charitable purpose.

6.20 The answer to whether the cy-près doctrine applies depends on whether there was **initial failure** or **subsequent failure**. Where there is an **initial failure**, there has to be a **general charitable intention** expressed in the trust deed. Therefore, a gift to a particular Catholic Seminary in **Re Rymer (1895)** which had ceased to exist by the date of the gift, failed as it could not be interpreted as being for the education of priests generally, and hence did not have a *general charitable intention* so could not be applied cy-près.

6.21 If the charitable trust failure is a **subsequent failure**, then the funds remaining **will be applied cy-près**.

CHAPTER 7
UNINCORPORATED
ASSOCIATIONS

Introduction

7.01 Unincorporated Associations occupy a curious place in English law. They have no legal personality, so technically do not exist, but play an important role in allowing clubs and societies to flourish. This chapter considers unincorporated associations and reflects on their position in English law.

7.02 The definition of an unincorporated association was given in the case of **Conservative and Unionist Central Office v Burrell (1982)**. It has the following key elements:

- two or more persons;

- bound together for one or more (non-business) purposes;

- with mutual undertakings;

- with mutual rights and obligations;

- may be joined and left at will.

Interpreting gifts to a UA

7.03 There is nothing difficult in the definition of an unincorporated association, but problems arise because UAs are not incorporated, ie, they are not an entity in their own right. An unincorporated association only exists as long as it has members. An unincorporated association cannot sue or be sued in its own name; it might only do so in the name of officers of the association. Therefore, how is it possible to make a gift to an association which does not have a separate legal personality? Members of unincorporated associations quite often want to leave a legacy (gift by will), to the UA of which they were a member. Well, what English law does is interpret those gifts in a method consistent with the wording chosen. There are five possible alternative interpretations, but the interpretation which has the most favoured is the 'contractual analysis'. Where the courts can do, they will interpret the gift in this way.

Aids to interpretation

7.04 As an aid to interpretation, the courts have developed principles which can assist in this task. They look at: (a) the size of the gift; (b) the number of recipients; (c) the type of property.

(a) gift to the members as joint tenants and tenants in common;

7.05 This interpretation operates as a gift to each individual member of the club and the club is used as a convenient label by which to identify the members of the association. This is generally restricted to smaller clubs, the example given by Vinelott J in **Re Grant (1980)** is that of a dining club. This interpretation does not further the purposes of the association; it merely operates as an outright gift to each member of the association. Under this interpretation, each member may use the funds for whatever they choose: purchase a car, go on holiday, and so on. Technically, such groups are not unincorporated associations because they do not satisfy the definition.

(b) trust for the purposes of the association;

7.06 Simply, this would be a void purpose trust and unenforceable in English law. This interpretation should be avoided, and any solicitor worth his salary should not draft a gift this way, or at least warn the testator of the consequences.

(c) trust for present and future members;

7.07 This interpretation is a people trust, but meets with a problem in English law; perpetuity. All trust interests in trusts for humans should vest within the perpetuity period, but the problem with clubs is that they have fluid membership, and they could go on forever. A trust for such a class of beneficiaries at common law would be void because an interest might vest outside the perpetuity period. The position was modified by statute. For trusts created after 15th July 1964 but before 6th April 2010, the Perpetuities and Accumulations Act 1964 gives a 'wait and see' period of 80 years, after which time the class closes, and those who are members of the club at that date will be the class of beneficiaries. For trusts created on or after 6th April 2010, the same principles apply, only the length of time is 125 years. Note: These provisions do not apply to the private purpose trusts in chapter six.

(d) gift to the members subject to the rules of the club ('the contractual analysis'/'contract holding theory')

7.08 Where the courts can interpret a gift to a club in this way, they will (**Universe Tankships of Monrovia v ITWF (1982)**). The 'contractual analysis' is the method which the courts have found to get around the difficulties which English trusts law has with gifts to unincorporated associations. So, how does it work? First, it is interpreted as a gift to the members which vests in them immediately. Secondly, the members of the club (who are bound by a contract with each other when they become members of the association), agree to use the property in accordance with the rules of the club. Therefore they are not free to use it as they please, that is, they can't take their money and run. The contractual analysis was first mooted by **Neville Estates v Madden (1962)**, and considered obiter in **Re Recher (1972)**.

7.09 In order for the court to be able to interpret a gift to an unincorporated association, a number of conditions operate. First, it must be possible to interpret the gift in this way. Secondly, there must be no stipulation in the gift which requires that the gift be used for a particular purpose. Thirdly, the club rules must give the association power to deal with the property in any way they like. Let's take each of these in turn.

(1) It must be possible to interpret the gift in this way

7.10 The language of the gift should be such as to make the interpretation possible. Therefore, language which sounds like a purpose trust is being created is not likely to lead to this interpretation.

(2) There must be no stipulation in the gift which requires that the gift be used for a particular purpose

7.11 A gift is a gift; the donor cannot give with one hand, but only hand the property over once you have agreed that the funds will be spent as he would like. Therefore, the following clause might not be possible to interpret under the 'contractual analysis': '£100,000 to the London Writers' Association for the sole purpose of renovating their London premises'. Here, the donor wishes to stipulate on what the funds will be spent. The courts have not always found this stipulation fatal to the contractual analysis interpretation. In **Re Lipinski (1976)**, the court interpreted a gift under the contractual analysis even with the words, 'to be used solely for the purposes of'. If the court can dismiss the language as a motive for the gift, it seems prepared to do so.

(3) The club rules must give the association power to deal with property in any way they like

7.12 If the club is limited by its rules in what it can do with the gift, usually because of some external control, then the gift will fail under the contractual analysis. In **Re Grant (1980)**, a bequest was left to a local branch of the Labour Party, but because each local Labour Party was subject to control from the national Labour Party, the gift failed. This was interpreted to mean that any external control renders the contractual interpretation impossible, but this was recently challenged in **Re Horley Town Football Club (2006)**. In this case, a limited degree of external control was not fatal to a finding that the gift took effect under the contractual analysis.

(e) Re Denley style trust

7.13 The **Re Denley** style of a trust is one which is for a designated purpose but which actually benefits identifiable individuals. In Re Denley, land was given to trustees to be held on trust for the purpose of providing a recreation or sports ground for the employees of a company and some others. This trust, though it was expressed as a purpose, actually benefited identifiable individuals who could enforce the trust by injunction (if necessary). However, for this analysis, there needs to be a perpetuity period. This is discussion in more detail in 5.08 – 5.10, above.

(f) Other interpretations

- Mandate theory

7.14 This theory comes, obiter, from the Court of Appeal in **Conservative and Unionist Central Office v Burrell (1982)**. Essentially, the members give the Treasurer a mandate to add the funds to the association and, once achieved, the mandate is irrevocable. The mandate theory has a very limited role.

Dissolution of UAs

7.15 What should happen to the assets of a UA when the members decide to close it down? The answer to this question should be simple, but it is actually a little more complicated than it first seems. Essentially, there are three options: (i) Distribution between the members; (ii) Bona vacantia to the Crown; (iii) Resulting Trust analysis.

(i) Distribution between members

7.16 If we embrace the contractual analysis, then on dissolution, the assets of the association should be distributed between the members of the association at the date of the dissolution (**Re Bucks Constabulary Widows' and Orphans' Fund (1979)**). This should be so irrespective of the source of the funds, eg, whether they came from member contributions, the general public through fundraising or raffles, or individual bequests. This is simple, intuitive, and logical, especially when one considers that the whole point of the contractual analysis is that the property becomes the members' property to do with as they please subject to the rules of the club. The primary basis for distribution is equal distribution, unless the rules of the club dictate a contrary basis for distribution.

(ii) Bona vacantia

7.17 That property should go bona vacantia to the Crown used to be limited to those situations where there was only one surviving member on the basis that a UA cannot exist with only one member (the UA was moribund), but since the case of **Hanchett-Stamford v Attorney-General (2008)**, the surviving member of the UA takes all property of the association absolutely. Bona vacantia may now be reserved only for those cases where it is impossible to determine who was the last surviving member of a UA, but such cases should be rare.

(iii) Resulting Trust

7.18 The resulting trust should be reserved for those gifts which are interpreted under the **Re Denley** analysis where there has been no nominated gift over in default at the end of the designated perpetuity period.

CHAPTER 8
IMPLIED TRUSTS

Introduction

8.01 A significant portion of the law of trusts is concerned with implied trusts. Implied trusts are not expressly created, rather they arise by operation of law. There are two forms of implied trust: the **constructive trust** and the **resulting trust**.

Constructive Trust

8.02 The constructive trust is imposed by law in response to established facts; not because of the intention of the parties.

8.03 In English law, the constructive trust is an **institution**; it responds to set circumstances requiring the wrongdoer to hold property on trust, constructive trust, for the victim. The trust is not intended, it is imposed because of the wrong which has been committed. However, in other jurisdictions, notably Canada, the constructive trust is a remedy, the **remedial constructive trust**, which allows the judge considerable freedom to distribute property rights between parties to do justice; the constructive trust as a remedy is discretionary.

8.04 Though the remedial constructive trust is not permitted in English law, the closest English law comes to recognising something similar is in implied trusts of the home. This is discussed in detail in chapter 9.

8.05 The main difference between the constructive trust as an 'institution' and as a 'remedy' is that the institutional constructive trust is said already to exist and the judge merely confirms its existence. In contrast, the remedial constructive trust operates from the date of judgment.

When does a constructive trust arise?

8.06 A constructive trust can arise in a wide range of circumstances. For example, it commonly arises where fraud is committed by the wrongdoer, but might also arise where the wrongdoer takes bribes (**Attorney-General for Hong-Kong v Reid (1994)(PC)**), or receives a secret profit (**FHR European Ventures LLP v Cedar Capital Partners LLC (2014)(SC)**). In **Keech v Sandford (1726)**, a constructive trust was imposed on a trustee when he attempted to renew a lease, which was formerly trust property, for himself.

8.07 Less controversially, a constructive trust might also arise during the purchase of land. After exchange of contracts, but before completion, a constructive trust is said to arise between the buyer and the seller. The seller is the trustee and the buyer is the beneficiary.

Resulting Trusts

8.08 In English law, there are two types of resulting trust: the presumed resulting trust and the automatic resulting trust (**Re Vandervell's Trusts (No. 2) (1974)**).

Presumed Resulting Trust

8.09 The presumed resulting trust tends to arise in two separate circumstances:

 i) Where there has been a voluntary conveyance of property;

 ii) Purchase money resulting trust.

i) Voluntary conveyance

8.10 A voluntary conveyance is where an individual has given property to another for no consideration; for nothing in return. Equity presumes against a gift because *equity will not assist a volunteer*. Therefore, a transfer from one party to another in the absence of consideration is presumed as a resulting trust for the transferor *unless* a gift or loan was intended. Evidence a gift or loan was intended will rebut the presumption of a resulting trust.

8.11 Note, the presumption of advancement will also rebut the presumption of a resulting trust. The presumption of advancement operates as between a husband and wife and parent and child, even where the child is an adult child (**Watkin v Watkin (2019)**). Thus, for example, a father giving money to a son or daughter will be presumed to be advancing that child by the payment. Advancement means to set the child up in life. The presumption of advancement will be abolished once s199, Equality Act 2010 comes into force. As of 1st January 2019, this statutory provision is not in force.

8.12 The presumption of a resulting trust is not abolished in relation to land merely because of the operation of s60(3), Law of Property Act 1925 (**Lohia v Lohia (2001)**). Of course, this much is clear from the case of **Hodgson v Marks (1971)**, where the presumed resulting trust arose in relation to land in that case (see paragraph 3.08, above).

ii)   Purchase money resulting trust

8.13 The presumed resulting trust will also operate where property is purchased in the name of one person, but the purchase money was provided by another (**Abrahams v Trustee in Bankruptcy of Abrahams (1999)**). If property is purchased using A's money, it is presumed that A will have a beneficial interest in the purchase by a resulting trust even though the legal title to the property is registered in B's name.

8.14 The presumption of a resulting trust in relation to the provision of purchase money for the purchase of **land** seems no longer to apply in domestic family homes cases (**Stack v Dowden (2007)**; **Jones v Kernott (2011)**). However, it does seem still to have a role in the commercial purchase of land or where land is purchased as a buy-to-let investment between family members (**Laskar v Laskar (2008)**), or where an agreement is made on the understanding that though the property goes into one party's name, the other party is intended to be beneficially entitled (**Tahir v Faizi (2019)**).

8.15 One final unusual point is that s3(2), Law Reform (Miscellaneous Provisions) Act 1970 presumes that an engagement ring passed between parties in a relationship is presumed to be a gift, unless the ring is given on express or implied condition that it should be returned if the marriage does not take place. An example of an implied condition would be where the engagement ring is a family heirloom.

Automatic Resulting Trust

8.16 An automatic resulting trust usually arises where an express trust has been attempted but fails.

8.17 A good example of an express trust is the case of **Vandervell v IRC (1967)** (discussed in chapter 3, 3.14 – 3.19). In that case, Vandervell failed to explain who, out of his employees or his grandchildren, would take the benefit of some shares. Consequently, the trust was void for uncertainty of object and the beneficial interest returned to Vandervell by automatic resulting trust.

8.18 A further example would be a trust declared **to A for life**. In such a case, when A dies, since there is no provision for what is to happen to the remainder after A's death, the property would return to the settlor by automatic resulting trust. Property cannot exist in suspense so it is simply returned to the party who gave it away.

8.19 In some circumstances, where a donation has been made for some purpose, and the purpose complete, then the automatic resulting trust will also operate to take the unused funds to the parties who donated them (**Re Abbott Fund (1900)**). However, while this works well with named and identified donations, it does not work well with anonymous donations, though the courts have insisted on applying it (**Re Gillingham Bus Disaster (1958)**).

CHAPTER 9
TRUSTS OF THE HOME

Introduction

9.01 Trusts of the home has undergone radical judicial reform since the decision of the House of Lords in **Stack v Dowden (2007)**. This decision, together with the Supreme Court decision of **Jones v Kernott (2011)**, and the cases which have subsequently applied both, mean the question of home ownership can now be approached more flexibly than in the past.

Background

9.02 If married or in a civil partnership, statute confers broad discretionary powers on judges to resolve questions of ownership of property, namely the Matrimonial Causes Act 1973 and the Civil Partnerships Act 2004, respectively. But what happens when couples are not in a formal relationship and later separate? What happens when such couples buy a house together? Or, one moves into the other's house?

9.03 This is an important social question because an increasing number of couples are declining to formalise their relationship. So, how does English law provide a solution? Well, the trust has been manipulated over the years in order to find a solution to the problem.

9.04 The starting point is to distinguish between cases where both parties are registered as the legal owners, so-called **joint names cases**, from those where only one of the parties is registered as the owner, namely, **single name cases**.

Express Declaration: Joint Names

9.05 Where the land has **joint legal owners**, then on transfer the TR1 land transfer form, part 10, provides the parties with an opportunity to declare their equitable ownership. They can be (a) **joint tenants**, (b) **tenants in common in equal shares**, or, (c) **hold it another way as they may stipulate**, where the parties can indicate their individual shares. Where this is done, it will be binding, even where one party has provided all the purchase money, but the property is conveyed to them as 'joint tenants' (**R v Hayes (2018)(CA)**).

9.06 It is not compulsory to complete this part of the TR1, and this generates problems. Baroness Hale in **Stack v Dowden (2007)(HL)** considered it should be compulsory. Indeed, she is not the first judge to bemoan the failure to complete part 10. If you want to see a judge 'shout' in a judgment, with the statement in upper case letters, take some time to read the immensely entertaining paragraph 44 of Ward LJ's judgment in **Carlton v Goodman (2002)(CA)**.

Express Declaration: Single Name

9.07 Where there is a **single legal owner**, ie, only one name is registered, a declaration of an express trust in favour of the non-legal owner would need to comply with **section 53(1)(b), Law of Property Act 1925**. This requires that the declaration be **evidenced by signed writing**. If this occurs, then the non-legal owner will have an enforceable beneficial interest. This could be done at the date of the conveyance or at a later date.

9.08 An express declaration is *generally* conclusive (**Pettitt v Pettitt (1969)**; **Goodman v Gallant (1986)**). In the case of **Pankhania v Chandegra (2012)**, the court declined to set aside an express trust unless there was **fraud, mistake**, or **undue influence**, though the earlier case of **Clarke v Meadus (2010)** permitted an express trust to be overridden by **proprietary estoppel**.

9.09 If there is no express declaration of trust, the **implied trust** (**Hodgson v Marks (1971)**) or **proprietary estoppel** offer alternative solutions.

Implied Trusts

9.10 Two forms of implied trust are relevant for the rest of our discussion: the **resulting trust** and the **constructive trust**. It is worthwhile taking some time to think about such trusts

Resulting Trust

9.11 The **presumed resulting trust** used to play a significant role in allowing a party to establish an equitable interest in the home. This would arise where one party **provided the purchase money at the point of acquisition** but, for whatever reason, the legal title to the property would go into another's name. The party providing the purchase money would receive a beneficial interest in the land (**Bull v Bull (1955)**).

9.12 However, the presumption of a resulting trust came in for criticism in the family home context because of its focus on financial contributions, ignoring all other contributions. Given this, the House of Lords in **Stack v Dowden (2007)** and the Supreme Court in **Jones v Kernott (2011)** stated that the presumption of a resulting trust is **not appropriate in the domestic family home context**, though it may have some value in other scenarios, eg, a house purchase made by members of the same family for purposes of a buy-to-let investment (**Laskar v Laskar (2008)(CA)**).

Constructive Trust

9.13 The constructive trust, though not traditionally used as a means of informally allocating ownership of the family home, began to be turned to this use in the middle of the 20th century. It has since been stretched as a concept, but is now the principal mechanism used in this area of law.

Joint Names

9.14 If joint legal owners of land fail to declare how the beneficial interests are held, by filling out part 10 of the TR1 (see 9.05, above), the starting point is **joint beneficial ownership** between the parties (**Stack v Dowden (2007)**; **Jones v Kernott (2011)**), **both parties have an equal (50:50) equitable interest because they have a legal interest**. **Joint beneficial ownership is a presumption** which can be rebutted. Rebutting the presumption is difficult (per Lord Walker in **Stack v Dowden (2007)**), but it may be done at two stages:

a) At the **point of acquisition** to show their common intention that a different beneficial ownership was intended; OR

b) That the parties **later** changed their common intention in relation to beneficial ownership.

9.15 There are two questions to determine in joint names cases: First, do the parties have a common intention to vary the starting point of 50:50? If so, secondly, then what is the amount each party is to receive? This two-stage approach was approved in **Barnes v Phillips (2015)(CA)**.

Common intention to vary 50:50?

9.16 To determine if the common intention of the parties has changed, either at the point of acquisition *or* subsequently, the task is to look for the **actual intention** of the parties to vary 50:50, or to infer from their conduct a common intention to vary 50:50, either initially or subsequently.

9.17 In **Jones v Kernott (2011)**, the parties cashed in life insurance policies so Mr Kernott could afford to move out of the family home and purchase his own house. From that point, Ms Jones made all the payments in respect of the joint home, ie, the mortgage, the utility bills, and so on. Thus, the common intention varied at that later date.

9.18 Also, in **Barnes v Phillips (2015)(CA)**, a subsequent remortgage was entirely to the benefit of Mr Barnes and that after 2008, Ms Phillips made all the mortgage payments. Thus, it could be inferred from their conduct that there was a common intention to vary 50:50 ownership.

9.19 The factors relevant to determining changes in the common intention of the parties are set down in paragraph 69 of Baroness Hale's speech in **Stack v Dowden (2007)**:

- Advice received by the parties, or discussions which they had at the point of purchase;

- The purpose for which the property was purchased;

- Their motivation for purchasing the property jointly;

- The nature of the relationship between the parties;

- Whether there are children of the relationship for which the parties have a responsibility to provide a home;

- The way in which the parties arranged their finances, eg, did they have separate bank accounts?;

- The way in which the couple paid bills and other outgoings in relation to the property;

- Why one party was authorised to give a valid receipt for capital monies.

9.20 All these factors are equal, where one is not superior to another. However, in some cases, like **Stack v Dowden (2007)**, the courts have given significant weight to financial contributions in departing from 50:50, though the facts of that case are unique. In contrast, in **Fowler v Barron (2008)**, one party contributed nothing towards the purchase of the property either in terms of a deposit or mortgage payments, yet the court did **not** allow the presumption of joint beneficial ownership to be rebutted.

What amount is each party to receive?

9.21 One should start the inquiry as to how much by considering if it can be worked out from the actual or inferred (drawing on the factors in para 69 of Stack v Dowden (2007)) common intention of the parties. If not, then it is possible to **impute their fair share having regard to their whole course of dealing in relation to the property**. An **imputed intention** is one the parties never actually had, but is one which the court believes is fair (**Jones v Kernott (2011)**, approving **Oxley v Hiscocks (2004)(CA)**). This approach was confirmed by the Court of Appeal in **Barnes v Phillips (2015)**.

9.22 Imputing a share based on what is fair has been criticised as arbitrary and tending to produce inconsistencies (**Aspden v Elvy (2012)**), but it now seems reasonably well-established.

Single Name

9.23 Where one name is on the legal title, the presumption is that the legal owner owns the entire beneficial interest: **one legal owner, one beneficial owner**. A party claiming an interest (that is, the non-legal owner) will need to do two things:

a) Show that they have an interest in the land (**'acquisition issue'**); AND,

b) The size of that interest (**'quantification issue'**).

9.24 This can be done by showing an express declaration of trust to comply with s53(1)(b), LPA 1925 (see, paras 9.07 – 9.08, above), or demonstrating that an implied trust exists, because s53(2), LPA 1925 suspends the formalities of s53(1)(b), LPA 1925 for such trusts. The two forms of implied trust are the resulting trust and the constructive trust, mentioned above at 9.10 – 9.13.

9.25 As indicated, the resulting trust has limited role in the domestic family home context (**Stack v Dowden (2007)**; **Jones v Kernott (2011)**), though it seems to remain for other situations (**Laskar v Laskar (2008)**). Consequently, we are really only concerned with the **constructive trust**.

9.26 For our purposes, there are two types of constructive trust: **express common intention constructive trust** ('**ECICT**'); and, **inferred common intention constructive trust ('ICICT') (Lloyd's Bank v Rosset (1991))**.

'acquisition issue': **ECICT**

9.27 The ECICT requires two things:

(i) Express agreement, arrangement, or understanding in relation to ownership of the land; AND

(ii) Detrimental reliance by the non-legal owner on the agreement, etc.

9.28 The express agreement as to ownership should be at the time of the purchase or *exceptionally* at some later date **(Lloyds Bank v Rosset (1991))** and communicated between the parties (**Springette v Defoe (1992)**). The agreement has to relate to ownership of the land, not merely sharing it as a home. Therefore, in **Clough v Killey (1996)**, a statement that everything was shared '50:50' was sufficient, as was a commitment that everything was 'half yours' in **Hammond v Mitchell (1992)**.

9.29 Somewhat unusually, the courts have also allowed 'excuses' made by the legal owner to constitute an agreement. In such cases, the legal owner will make an excuse for **not** putting the non-legal owner on the legal title. For example, stating that the non-legal owner is 'too young' as in **Eves v Eves (1974)**, that any inclusion might prejudice a divorce settlement, as in **Grant v Edwards (1986)**, or that there are tax implications from being on legal title as in **Hammond v Mitchell (1992)**. In **Curran v Collins (2015)**, where the excuse related to the expense of two names being on the legal title, the court indicated that interpretation of the excuse is fact-sensitive, but should generally be coupled with a positive assertion the property would be jointly owned.

9.30 The express agreement should be followed by detrimental reliance (**Lloyds Bank v Rosset (1991)**; **Eves v Eves (1974)**). This is conduct which cannot otherwise be explained: why did they do it if they didn't think they were getting an interest in the property? (**Grant v Edwards (1986)**).

9.31 Detriment includes improvements to the family home (**Eves v Eves (1970)**), or indirect financial contributions to the household, without which, the legal owner could not pay the mortgage (**Grant v Edwards (1986)**; and in the ICICT context, **Le Foe v Le Foe (2001)**). Minor amendments and decoration (**Pettitt v Pettitt (1970)**) do not count as detrimental reliance.

'quantification issue': ECICT

9.32 Where there is an express agreement which makes clear the share each party is to have, *generally* that will be given effect. So, in **Clough v Killey (1992)** and **Hammond v Mitchell (1992)**, the parties were given half each. In **Williamson v Sheikh (2008)**, the court used an unsigned trust deed to determine the agreed share. However, where there has been express agreement as to ownership, but no statement as to the shares, it may be possible to infer an agreement. In **Gallarotti v Sebastianelli (2012)**, two friends bought a property together with an express agreement as to 50:50. This was later varied by inference that they were to share the property other than equally where S was awarded a greater share (75%) to account for the fact that S paid the mortgage contributions alone.

9.33 However, if there is no expressly agreed share, and it is not possible to infer from their conduct, then it may be possible for the court to impute shares where it is considered **fair having regard to the whole course of dealing between them in relation to the property**.

'acquisition issue': **ICICT**

9.34 Where there is no express common intention, it is possible to drawn an inference to share ownership from the parties' conduct in relation to the property. In **Lloyds Bank v Rosset (1991)**, Lord Bridge indicated that *only* contributions to mortgage payments would be sufficient to give rise to the inference. However, Baroness Hale in **Stack v Dowden (2007)** stated that set the threshold too high and that the **law had moved on** from that position.

9.35 It is possible that indirect financial contributions are sufficient if they are referable to the acquisition of the property (**Gissing v Gissing (1968)**). Also, where the contributions are to payment of bills, without which, the legal owner would not be able to afford the mortgage, then this may suffice (**Le Foe v Le Foe (2001)**). This is sometimes referred to as the 'family economy thesis'.

9.36 Further, substantial improvement to the property by DIY might be enough to infer an agreement to share ownership (obiter in **Stack v Dowden (2007)**). Also, in **Aspden v Elvy (2012)**, an inference was found where the direct financial contributions were made to the conversion of the property, rather than to its acquisition.

9.37 Perhaps the most significant development is the suggestion in the Privy Council case of **Abbott v Abbott (2007)** that the full range of paragraph 69 factors from **Stack v Dowden (2007)** (see, para 9.19, above), might be used when seeking to draw an inference as to sharing ownership of the home.

9.38 Before turning to the issue of quantification, it is worth noting that it is not possible to impute at this stage in the process, ie, 'acquisition' (**Capethorn v Harris (2015)(CA)**).

'quantification issue': **ICICT**

9.39 Generally, the inference will generate the amount to be shared. So, if the inference is equality, that will be the position. However, if nothing can be inferred, then, and only then, may the court impute by **having regard to the whole course of dealing between the parties in relation to the property** (**Oxley v Hiscocks (2004)**, approved in **Jones v Kernott (2011)**). This approach was taken in **Thompson v Hurst (2012)**, **Aspden v Elvy (2012)**, and **Graham-York v York (2015)**.

Proprietary Estoppel

9.40 A further means of establishing an interest in the home and which was certainly in prominent use prior to the changes made to the law by **Stack v Dowden (2007)** and **Jones v Kernott (2011)**, is proprietary estoppel. Prior to the changes brought about by Stack and Jones, proprietary estoppel offered a basis for reforming the law in this area (**Law Commission, Sharing Homes: Discussion Paper, Law Com No 278 (2002)**).

9.41 In **Thorner v Major (2009)(HL)**, it was stated that in order to establish proprietary estoppel, the claimant needed to show:

a)   a representation made or assurance given to the claimant;

b)   reliance by the claimant on the representation or assurance; and,

c)   some detriment incurred by the claimant as a consequence of that reliance.

9.42 The assurance could be a clear representation, or passive encouragement. Clearly, the detriment would be fact-sensitive and not something which is limited to financial expenditure in reliance on the assurance.

9.43 In respect of remedy, the claimant will not necessarily receive what was promised in the assurance, though this is possible. The remedy will depend on the claimant's expectation and the detriment suffered, including the context. For example, in **Pascoe v Turner (1979)**, though the claimant's detriment was small, in the context of the claimant's overall (limited) wealth, it was in fact a significant detriment.

Reform

9.44 It is certainly the case that the law has been significantly reformed by judicial action since the decision of the House of Lords in **Stack v Dowden (2007)**, but is this the end of the matter? Possibly not. There has been an increase in cases before the courts since **Stack** as its limits are explored in order to produce settled principles. However, an approach which has 'fairness' in it will always result in some degree of uncertainty in case law, though it is doubtful a comprehensive statutory regime would produce a system which is any better as it would still need to be discretionary. This is the problem with an area of law such as this one. Legal rules and principles which are too strict may result in some semblance of injustice, as in **Burns v Burns (1984)**, whereas a system which places reasonable discretion in the hands of the judiciary may be difficult to apply consistently from case to case.

CHAPTER 10
TRUSTEESHIP AND TRUSTEES' POWERS AND DUTIES

Introduction

10.01   The office of trustee is an onerous one and should not be undertaken lightly. Once appointed, a trustee assumes obligations (duties) towards the trustee and a personal liability where those obligations are breached. This means that the trustee is liable to the full extent of their estate. In addition to duties, trustees are also given a range of powers. This chapter is about those duties and powers.

Appointment, Retirement and Removal of Trustees

10.02   The settlor, the person creating the trust, should give careful consideration to the appointment of a trustee. The trustee should be, at the very least, trustworthy, but they should also be competent in a range of matters from simple administration to more complex issues of investment.

Capacity

10.03   Anyone with the capacity to hold property may be a trustee. A minor cannot be a trustee, even where the trust property is personal property (**s20, Law of Property Act 1925**).

Number of Trustees

10.04   A trust might operate with only **one trustee**. Though there is technically no upper limit on the number, a trust of land may have no more than four trustees (**s34, Trustee Act 1925**). It is wise not to have too many trustees, especially since they must act unanimously, unless the trust deed permits majority decisions (**Staechelin v ACLBDD Holdings Ltd (2019)**). Two trustees has practical advantages: Two trustees can keep an eye on each other, discuss decisions respecting the trust and, further, having two trustees allows overreaching to occur.

Appointment of Original Trustees

10.05   Original trustees are *generally* appointed by the trust deed. If not, a court application is made to appoint trustees. This is either under the **court's inherent jurisdiction**, the **Judicial Trustees Act 1896**, or the **Trustee Act 1925**.

10.06   The trustee must have notice of the trust and expressly or impliedly accept the trusteeship (**Robinson v Pett (1734)**).

Replacement of Original Trustees

10.07   It is perhaps obvious that the original trustees might need to be replaced, either because of illness, old age, or because they move out of the country. In such circumstances, it is possible that the trust deed contains powers as to the replacement of trustees, otherwise, there are significant statutory powers.

Section 36, Trustee Act 1925

10.08   Section 36, Trustee Act 1925 provides that certain persons may appoint trustees where a trustee is dead, remains outside United Kingdom for more than 12 months, the trustee wishes no longer to remain a trustee, the trustee is unfit to act, or the trustee is a minor. The final circumstance would be very rare, though could occur in the context of a resulting trust (**Re Vinogradoff (1935)**).

Section 41, Trustee Act 1925

10.09   A court can appoint trustees where, without the court's assistance, it would be **inexpedient**, **difficult**, or **impracticable** to do so.

Section 19, Trusts of Land and Appointment of Trustees Act 1996

10.10   Beneficiaries may appoint trustees under s19, Trusts of Land and Appointment of Trustees Act 1996, provided all beneficiaries are of **full age**, **together absolutely entitled**, and **agree unanimously** to the suggested appointment.

End of Trusteeship

10.11   Trusteeship naturally ends on the death of the trustee, but can end by retirement of the trustee. If there is a power in the trust deed permitting retirement then this is possible, or where a retiring trustee is being replaced with a new trustee (s36, Trustee Act 1925). Under s39, Trustee Act 1925, it is possible for a trustee to retire without a replacement appointed provided it is done by deed, the consent of co-trustees is received by deed, and two trustees or a trust corporation remain in place. Retirement might also be by court order under s41, Trustee Act 1925 or by the beneficiaries under s19, Trusts of Land and Appointment of Trustees Act 1996.

10.12   Trusteeship might also end by the bankruptcy of the trustee or by the trustee's impropriety, eg, the trustee misappropriates trust property or commits a fraud on the beneficiaries.

Distinction between Powers and Duties

10.13   When appointed to the office of trustee, trustees are given certain powers and made the subject of certain duties. A power is something which trustees have the ability to do, but not the obligation to do. A duty, on the other hand, is something which the trustees must undertake. Sometimes, the two interact. For example, trustees are under a duty to invest the trust property, but the powers over what they might invest in vary from trust to trust. Sometimes the power is quite extensive (as, for example, under s3, Trustee Act 2000), and sometimes restricted (as, for example, where the trustees might not have the power to invest in armaments manufacture).

Trustee Powers

10.14   As indicated, powers vary from trust to trust. A well drafted trust deed will provide the trustees with extensive powers which will undoubtedly assist in their management of the trust fund. Where trust powers are not contained in the trust deed, there are some circumstances in which the trust powers will be imposed by statute. For example, trustee powers over use of income and capital (**ss31** and **32, Trustee At 1925**).

10.15   Trustees will often enjoy a power of sale over trust assets. This is generally expressly stated in the trust deed. If a trust asset is not performing adequately in terms of producing an income, it might be better to sell it to invest the proceeds of sale in some other asset.

10.16   Trustees also have the power, ie, the ability, to insure the trust property. Note, there is no duty to insure the trust property. However, a trustee might see insuring the trust property as a sensible course of action, especially if the trust property is land.

10.17   An important power which trustees now have is the power to delegate some of their functions. A well-drafted trust deed will contain the power to delegate, but under the general law it was not possible to delegate functions once appointed to the office of trustee. However, following changes introduced by the Trustee Act 2000, it is **now possible to delegate a wide range of matters, including investment decisions**. A trustee would do well to bear in mind the costs implications of delegating functions to an agent.

10.18 Finally, trustees have important powers over the use to which the income and capital is put, usually during the minority of a beneficiary. It makes good practical sense to allow the trustee certain powers over the income of a trust for use of a minor beneficiary. For example, the income could be used for the education of the beneficiary. These powers, where not expressly contained in the trust deed, are contained in the Trustee Act 1925. These powers are discussed in detail in chapter 12.

Trustee Duties

10.19 Duties are obligations; they must be carried out. If the trustee fails to carry out their duties under a trust, this may result in a breach of trust for which the trustee is liable. **A trustee owes duties to the beneficiary**. Duties may be found in the trust deed, in statute, or under the general law.

10.20 The **general duty of care** is found in **s1, Trustee Act 2000** ('the statutory duty of care'). This may be excluded (**schedule 1, paragraph 7, TA 2000**), and where it is excluded the common law duty of care of the prudent man of business applies (**Speight v Gaunt (1889)**).

10.21 The statutory duty of care has objective and subjective elements. The trustee must exercise **such care and skill as is reasonable in the circumstances** ('the objective element'), having particular regard to **special knowledge or experience** he has or holds himself as having ('the subjective element'). Further, if the trustee acts in the course of a business or profession, regard should be had to any special knowledge or experience that it is reasonable to expect of a person acting in the course of that kind of business or profession.

10.22 Whether a trustee has discharged the duty of care which is imposed on him is a fact-sensitive inquiry which must be judged on a case-by-case basis. Breach is considered in chapter 13.

10.23   The trustees other significant duty is the duty of investment. Trustees have to invest the trust property; failure to do so is a breach of trust. This is discussed in chapter 11.

10.24   In addition to these main duties, trustees are subject to other duties:

Familiarise themselves with the terms of the trust	This is, perhaps, obvious. The trustee should know the extent of their powers and duties, and identify the beneficiaries. Indeed, it is in the interests of trustees to do this so they avoid attracting liability for breach of trust.
Obligation to safeguard the trust assets	This is a duty to see that the assets of the trust remain intact, that they do not suffer damage, etc. This might mean insuring the trust assets, though insuring is a trust power.
Distribute trust property in accordance with the terms of the trust	The trustee is under a duty to distribute the trust property in accordance with the trust instrument. Acting inconsistently by, for example, distributing trust property unequally between beneficiaries where it is supposed to be distributed equally is a breach of this duty.
Equality between beneficiaries	The trustees must treat beneficiaries equally, even where their interests are

	different. This is sometimes referred to as the duty to act even-handedly.
Balance the interests of different beneficiaries	This duty is linked to the previous one. The trustee, you will recall, is under a duty to treat beneficiaries equally, and the duty to balance the interests of different beneficiaries might be regarded as a facet of this duty. For example, if a trust is to A for life, remainder to B, A has an interest in the income and B an interest in the capital. The interests of both beneficiaries, even though different, should be balanced and treated in the same way; A should not be favoured over B and vice versa.
Accounts and Information	The trustee is under a duty to provide the sort of information to the beneficiary which they might need in order to check the performance of the trust. This includes providing accounts, and other relevant information.
Fiduciary nature of trusteeship	Trustees are fiduciaries. A fiduciary owes an obligation of loyalty to the beneficiary. This means that a trustee should not place their self-interest before the duty owed to the beneficiary. This

	is expressed in the prohibition on self-dealing (below). Fiduciary Duties are discussed in detail in chapter 14.

Self-dealing

10.25   As a general rule, the trustee is not permitted to purchase the trust property; this is known as self-dealing. The reason this is not permitted is that the trustee would be purchasing the property from himself as trustee. There may be a conflict of interest; as trustee he should be seeking the best price in the sale of trust property, whereas as the buyer, he might well be seeking the lowest price.

10.26   An exception might be where the trust property is sold to a company of which the trustee is a shareholder. This is because a company is a separate legal entity from the trustee. However, the question will often turn on whether the trustee is a majority or minority shareholder. If a majority shareholder, then this would be regarded as self-dealing and the transaction set aside (**Re Thompson (1985)**). If a minority shareholder, then the burden of proof is on the company to show that a fair value was paid (**Farrar v Farrars (1888)**).

10.27   An unusual case on authorised self-dealing is **Holder v Holder (1968)**. In this case, one of three executors of an estate was interested in purchasing trust property, a farm. The executor was open and honest about his intention, informed the parties, the purchase was made at auction, and at the material time the executor in question had only undertaken minor activities on behalf of the estate. Consequently, given the unusual facts of the case, the contract was upheld and the sale went ahead.

Fair dealing

10.28   Fair dealing is the purchase of the beneficiary's beneficial interest by the trustee. Fair dealing is less heavily regulated because there is no conflict of interest, unlike with self-dealing, because the trustee is trying to buy the beneficiary's beneficial interest from the beneficiary; there are two distinct parties to the contract. However, the onus is on the trustee to show there was no abuse of position by the trustee, that the beneficiary was fully informed and, finally, that the trustee paid fair value.

Directorships using trust shares

10.29   In some circumstances, it might be appropriate to appoint a trustee to the board of directors of a company where the trust property is a majority shareholding in that company (**Re Lucking (1968)**). However, a question which often arises is: Can the trustee-director retain fees which he is paid as a director? This depends on which shares appointed the trustee-director.

10.30   In **Re Macadam (1946)**, where trustees used a power which they had to appoint directors and appointed themselves, they were required to give up the fees they obtained as trustee-directors. However, if appointed without the trust's shareholding (**Re Gee (1948)**), or they were already directors before being appointed a trustee (**Re Dover Coalfield (1908)**), then the trustee-director can retain any fees paid.

Remuneration and reimbursement

10.31   Before discussing the detail, it is necessary to distinguish between remuneration and reimbursement. **Remuneration is the receipt of payment for undertaking the office of trustee**. Generally, the office of trustee is an unremunerated office; trustees should not receive payment. However, this is subject to exceptions, discussed below. **Reimbursement**, on the other hand, **is repayment of the trustee for expenses they have incurred in carrying out the functions on behalf of the trust**, eg, purchasing paper, making phone calls, etc. It is possible for a trustee to be reimbursed for their expenditure.

10.32   As indicated, the office of trustee is unremunerated, though this is subject to exceptions. First, where the trust deed contains a charging clause allowing trustees to charge for their services, the remuneration of trustees is permitted. Indeed, professional trustees will not generally act unless there is a charging clause in the trust deed. Secondly, where the beneficiary or the court (**Re Duke of Norfolk's ST (1982)**) authorises the remuneration of trustees, then the trustee may be paid. Thirdly, under **ss28** and **29, Trustee Act 2000**, the trustees may also be paid for carrying out their duties as trustee.

CHAPTER 11
INVESTMENT

Introduction

11.01 Trustees are under a **duty to invest the trust fund for the benefit of all the beneficiaries**, whether a life tenant or a remainderman. Therefore, trustees are also under a **duty to act even-handedly when investing**; generating an income for the life tenant and maintaining or increasing the capital value for the remainderman.

11.02 Though under a duty to invest, the power over what the trustees might invest in can vary from trust to trust. Investment powers are found in the **trust deed** (the document which creates the trust) or the **Trustee Act 2000 ('TA 2000')**. A professionally-drafted trust deed will have an investment clause, but where the trust deed is silent, the TA 2000 will operate.

11.03 A trustee must not leave trust money uninvested for an unreasonable period (**AG v Alford (1855)**); liability may arise if the trustee does so.

11.04 The TA 2000 came into force on 1st February 2001 and repealed the Trustee Investments Act 1961. It was thought the old law was out-of-date and not reflective of modern investment practice.

11.05 'Investment' was given a narrow meaning by the courts. In **Re Wragg (1919)**, it was interpreted to mean holding property for the income it would generate; something which had capital appreciation was not an 'investment'. However, this must no longer be regarded as good law. The provisions of the TA 2000 (in which investment is not defined), and the current theory of investment set down in **Nestle v National Westminster Bank plc (1993)**, suggest that an investment can either generate income or increase in value.

The Trustee Act 2000: The 'statutory duty of care'

11.06   Part I, TA 2000, imposes a new statutory duty of care. Under s1(1), TA 2000 a trustee must exercise such care and skill as is reasonable in all the circumstances, having regard in particular to (a) special knowledge or experience he has or holds himself out as having, and if he (b) acts as trustee in the course of a business or profession, to any special knowledge or experience that it is reasonable to expect of a person acting in the course of that kind of business or profession.

11.07   The statutory duty of care is a **two-part duty**: **partly subjective, partly objective**. Section 1(1)(a), TA 2000 looks, subjectively, at the status of the trustee, whereas s1(1)(b), TA 2000 looks at the professional trustee by the standards which might reasonably be expected of a professional, therefore is an objective test.

11.08   Section 2, TA 2000 directs to schedule 1 of the Act and the circumstances when the statutory duty of care applies to the trustee. The duty of care applies to a trustee:

- when exercising the general power of investment or any other power of investment

- when carrying out a duty relating to the exercise of the power of investment (s4, TA 2000)

- when carrying out a duty relating to the review of investments (s5, TA 2000)

- when exercising the power to acquire land (s8, TA 2000)

- when appointing or reviewing the appointment of an agent (s11, TA 2000; s22, TA 2000)

11.09   Under Sch 1, para 7, TA 2000, the statutory duty of care may be excluded by the trust instrument. If this occurs, the common law duty of care – the **prudent man of business (Speight v Gaunt (1883))** – applies.

Trustee Act 2000: 'General Power of Investment'

11.10   A trustee may make **any kind of investment he could make as if he were absolutely entitled to the assets of the trust**. By s6(1)(b), TA 2000, the **general power of investment ('GPI') can be excluded by the trust instrument**. The GPI in the TA 2000 is more reflective of investment powers drafted in practice.

11.11   The TA 2000 gives no definition of an 'investment'; case law must be relied upon. Traditionally, 'investment' meant property which produced an income (**Re Wragg (1919)**). This interpretation was regarded as too restrictive as ignoring the capital. The more modern approach to 'investment' comes from **Harries v Church Commissioners (1992)** which emphasised both income generation and capital growth.

11.12   Section 8, TA 2000 permits the trustees to **purchase land as an investment** (s8(1)(a), TA 2000), whether freehold or leasehold. Trustees may purchase land for the beneficiary to occupy (s8(1)(b), TA 2000), though land purchased for the beneficiary to occupy will not generate an income (because the beneficiary is living in it!)

Trustee Act 2000: 'Standard Investment Criteria'

11.13   In exercising *any* **power of investment**, whether under the Act or the trust instrument, a trustee must have regard to the **standard investment criteria ('SIC')** (s4, TA 2000). When reviewing investments, trustees must also have regard to the SIC. The SIC require the trustee to consider the **suitability** (s4(3)(a), TA 2000) of an investment and the need for **diversification** (s4(3)(b), TA 2000).

11.14   First, the trustee must consider the **suitability of the type of investment** under consideration, eg, shares. If suitable, the trustee must then consider whether the particular shares are appropriate to the circumstances of their trust. **Suitability is a relative concept**. What is suitable for one trust might not be suitable for another.

11.15   The need for **diversification** is statutory

recognition of the '**modern portfolio theory**' (**Nestle v National Westminster Bank plc (1993)**). The modern portfolio theory encourages diversification so the risks associated with investment are spread throughout the portfolio in case investments go bad. The need for diversification should reflect the circumstances of the particular trust.

Trustee Act 2000: Advice

11.16   When exercising any power of investment, or when reviewing investments, the trustee must **obtain and consider proper advice**. However, under s5(3), TA 2000, the trustee need not obtain advice if they **reasonably conclude it is not necessary**.

11.17   If they take advice, it must be the advice of a **person reasonably believed by the trustee to be qualified** to give it by reason of his **ability in and practical experience of financial** and other matters relating to the proposed investment (s5(4), TA 2000).

11.18   This is both a subjective and objective test. The belief must be genuine and reasonably held by the trustee.

Trustee Act 2000: Delegation

11.19   At common law, trustees were not permitted to delegate their functions; the trustee accepted the office of trustee, so they should carry out the tasks. This is no longer the position.

11.20   Under s11, TA 2000, trustees can delegate delegable functions to an agent.

11.21   'Delegable functions' include all functions, except:

  a)   distributive functions;

  b)   power to decide if expenditure comes out of capital or income;

c)   power to appoint a trustee.

11.22   Thus, the powers under ss31 and 32, Trustee Act 1925, cannot be delegated, nor powers of distribution under a discretionary trust, though **investment decisions can be delegated**.

11.23   The trustee may delegate to another trustee, but not to a beneficiary.

11.24   The agent is subject to the duties and restrictions in respect of what has been delegated to them.

11.25   The trustee must regularly review the arrangement with the agent (s22, TA 2000).

11.26   The trustee is not liable for the agent's default unless the trustee failed to comply with the statutory duty of care in appointing the agent or reviewing the arrangements with the agent (s23, TA 2000).

Ethical Investment

11.27   The trust fund should be invested for the best financial returns. This is a general rule.

11.28   In modern trusts, some wish moral and ethical considerations to be taken into account. While these are not generally permitted (**Cowan v Scargill (1985)**), if the trust deed expressly makes provision, or the beneficiaries consent to it, then it may be permitted.

11.29   Additionally, a charitable trust may limit its powers to purchase certain investments if it would be inconsistent with its purposes. For example, a cancer research charitable trust might not want to invest in cigarette manufacturers.

11.30   In **Bishop of Oxford v Church Commissioners for England (1992)** it was stated that ethical investment may be preferred to financial considerations if the ethical investment would bring the same return. This would be difficult to prove.

CHAPTER 12
MAINTENANCE AND
ADVANCEMENT

Introduction

12.01   You might wish to familiarise yourself with some of the terminology explained and defined in chapter 1 as much of that terminology is used again here.

12.02   Powers can be given to trustees by the trust deed or statute.

12.03   The powers of maintenance and advancement are powers given to trustees over the use of income and capital for the benefit of the beneficiary. Remember, the power to do something is the ability to do something, but not the obligation to do something.

12.04   The powers of maintenance and advancement, if none are provided by the trust deed, are contained in the Trustee Act 1925 ('TA 1925'). These powers are in addition to those in the trust deed and *only* apply if there is no contrary intention in the trust deed (s69(2), Trustee Act 1925).

12.05   The statutory powers of maintenance and advancement are contained in ss31 and 32, Trustee Act 1925. These powers may be varied by the trust deed.

12.06   The powers in ss31 relate to **income**; the powers in s32 relate to **capital**.

Section 31, Trustee Act 1925

12.07   Income is whatever is generated by the investment of the trust property. Section 31, Trustee Act 1925 gives trustees the power to use the income for a minor beneficiary (ie, below the age of 18), or accumulate it during minority. Accumulation of income means not using it; keeping it in reserve for (possible) future use.

Minor beneficiary

12.08   A minor beneficiary is one under the age of 18. A minor beneficiary has **no right to income during minority**. Under s31, trustees may use income for the '**maintenance, education** or **benefit**' of a minor beneficiary, whether the interest is **vested** or **contingent**.

12.09   Where money is used for the benefit of a minor beneficiary, it cannot be paid to the minor; **a minor cannot give a valid receipt**. Instead, the money must be used directly for purpose or paid to a parent or guardian for use in the beneficiary's interests.

12.10   Income not used **must be accumulated**, namely reinvested to produce further income (s31(2), TA 1925). Accumulated income may still be used for the beneficiary's maintenance.

12.11   When using income for the maintenance, education or benefit of a minor, trustees are required to take account of the beneficiary's age, requirements, and to their circumstances generally. Careful consideration should be given to exercise of the power; payments should not be automatic (**Wilson v Turner (1883)**). The power must be exercised in the interests of the minor beneficiary (**Fuller v Evans (2000)**).

Beneficiary of majority

12.12   When the beneficiary reaches 18, he becomes entitled to the income (**Stanley v IRC (1944)**), whether the interest is vested or contingent.

12.13   At 18, the beneficiary is **not automatically entitled** to **accumulated income**, unless the beneficiary:

   a)   Had a vested interest during his minority; OR

   b)   Acquires an absolute interest in capital at 18.

12.14 Otherwise, accumulations follow capital, that is, they stay with the capital.

Section 32, Trustee Act 1925

12.15 Section 32, TA 1925, gives trustees the power to use capital for the **advancement** or **benefit** of a beneficiary entitled to the capital, whether their interest is **absolute** or **contingent**, or in **possession** or **remainder**.

12.16 There is no age restriction on this provision.

12.17 The power of advancement is subject limitations. First, advancements should be taken into account when the beneficiary becomes absolutely entitled and, secondly, the power under s32, TA 1925 **cannot be used where there is a prior life interest ('life tenant')**, unless the life tenant gives their signed written consent (s32(1)(c), TA 1925).

12.18 Advancements used to be limited under s32 to only half of the presumptive share of capital. This restriction was removed by s8, Inheritance and Trustees' Powers Act 2014 so that now, the whole capital sum might be advanced. However, there are good practical reasons why a trustee would not necessarily do this for the beneficiary.

Advancement or benefit

12.19 'Advancement' means to **set the beneficiary up in life**. Examples include: Purchasing the beneficiary an Army commission (**Lawrie v Bankes (1858)**); purchasing surgery premises for a doctor-beneficiary (**Re Williams' WT (1953)**); paying the beneficiary's debts (**Lowther v Bentinck (1874)**); assisting the beneficiary in establishing a career as a barrister (**Roper-Curzon v Roper-Curzon (1871)**).

12.20 Section 32 allows resettlement of capital to create a new trust, but not so as to remove the interest of the beneficiary (**Pilkington v IRC (1964)**).

12.21 'Benefit' means to **improve the beneficiary's material situation**. The power of advancement has been held to apply where an advancement was made allowing the beneficiary to make a charitable donation. It discharged a moral obligation to give to charity which the beneficiary felt he had (**Re Clore (1966)**). Important to the decision in Re Clore was that the beneficiary was independently wealthy. It seems the principle will not apply where the beneficiary would not have their own funds to make such a charitable donation without the advancement of funds (**X v A (2005)**).

CHAPTER 13
BREACH OF TRUST AND REMEDIES

Introduction

13.01   The cause of action for breach of trust requires that there is a duty which is breached by the trustee. Whether the duty is breached is a complex question. Further, there are also causal requirements and, further, that the loss to the trust fund be demonstrated.

13.02   In order for the trustee to be liable, it must be shown, first, that there is a duty of care imposed upon them whether by the trust deed, by statute, or at common law. The statutory duty of care is in **s1, Trustee Act 2000 ('TA 2000')**. The statutory duty can be excluded (**Sch 1, para 7, TA 2000**) and, where it is, the common law duty of care continues to apply. This is the prudent man of business (**Speight v Gaunt (1883)**).

13.03   The statutory duty of care and, for that matter, the common law duty of care, do not require the trustee to be perfect; **trustees are human**, *not* **superhuman**. Nevertheless, if trustees go too far, they have to understand that liability may well attach to them for their actions or inactions.

13.04   Under s1(1), TA 2000 a trustee must exercise such care and skill as is reasonable in all the circumstances, having regard in particular to (a) special knowledge or experience he has or holds himself out as having, and if he (b) acts as trustee in the course of a business or profession, to any special knowledge or experience that it is reasonable to expect of a person acting in the course of that kind of business or profession.

13.05   The statutory duty of care is a **two-part duty**: **partly subjective, partly objective**. Section 1(1)(a), TA

2000 looks, subjectively, at the status of the trustee, whereas s1(1)(b), TA 2000 looks at the professional trustee by the standards which might reasonably be expected of a professional, therefore is an objective test.

13.06 This drafting seems to render a difference in approach between professional and lay trustees. *Generally*, professional trustees are expected to come to a higher standard than lay trustees. Professional trustees hold themselves out as having special skill and knowledge, they expect to be paid, and they often have professional indemnity insurance which helps deflect liability from them to their insurer.

Breach

13.07 It is important to be aware of different types of breach. There are straightforward breaches, such as where the trustee has to distribute trust property equally between beneficiaries and does not do so, and more complex breaches which are determined by whether the required standard has not been met. Unsurprisingly, it is the latter which are more contentious.

13.08 Useful cases to compare on whether the duty of care has been breached are **Re Lucking (1968)** and **Bartlett v Barclay's Bank (1980)**. Both cases concerned a trust fund which consisted of a majority shareholding in a private company. One of the issues in each case was how best to protect the interests of the trust. In Re Lucking it was said that where the trustees had the power to appoint themselves to the board of directors, then this should be done. This would see that trustees, as directors, could keep a better sense of how the company was doing and how it was being managed. By appointing themselves, the judge felt the duty of care would be discharged.

13.09 However, Bartlett suggested that it would be sufficient if the trustees were provided with minutes of board meetings and information relating to relevant business decisions. This way, they would be in a position to judge the performance of the company and identify any possible risks to it and, consequently, the trust's shareholding.

13.10 Both of these cases indicate the difference of opinion which can often exist where one is concerned with how best to protect the interests of the beneficiaries. They emphasise that the question will be one best determined by close analysis of the facts of the case.

Causation

13.11 When it comes to causation in trusts, it is much more straightforward than at common law. All the beneficiary need demonstrate is that there is some causal link between the breach of trust and the loss suffered.

Basic principle of trustee liability

13.12 In those cases where there is only one trustee, the approach to liability is relatively straightforward; the trustee is the person to sue for breach of trust. However, matters of liability are more complex where a trust has multiple trustees. Sometimes, the search for the truth of a transaction is more challenging where there are multiple trustees who might tend to seek to blame the other.

13.13 The starting point for liability of multiple trustees is **joint and several liability**. This means that multiple trustees are jointly liable for breach of trust, or they might be individually liable (several). This means that the beneficiary might sue both beneficiaries or any one of the trustees individually.

13.14 However, where one trustee is sued individually, that trustee might seek a contribution from the other trustee under the **Civil Liability (Contribution) Act 1978** which, by s6(1), applies to trustees. The 1978 Act gives courts a broad discretion to require a trustee to contribute **such sum as may be just and equitable** (s2(1)). Section 2(2) of the 1978 Act allows courts to give one trustee a complete indemnity.

This power is in addition to common law powers over indemnity, discussed below.

Indemnity

13.15   In cases where there are multiple trustees, one trustee can be required to indemnify the other. This means that the other trustee will not be liable to pay damages; they have an indemnity. An indemnity will be possible where one of the trustees has committed fraud (**Re Smith (1896)**), or where one of the trustees is a professional trustee and the other is a lay trustee (**Re Partington (1887)**). The lay trustee is generally protected by an indemnity, unless the lay trustee has also caused the breach (**Head v Gould (1898)**).

13.16   It is also possible that a trustee-beneficiary (that is, a beneficiary who is also a trustee), might also be liable to indemnify the other trustee. In such cases, the trustee-beneficiary may be required to indemnify the other trustee to the extent of their interest (**Chillingworth v Chambers (1896)**).

Section 61, Trustee Act 1925

13.17   Section 61, Trustee Act 1925 may operate to relieve, wholly or partially, (**Re Evans (1999)**) the trustee of liability for breach where the trustee is able to prove they acted **honestly**, **reasonably**, and **ought fairly to be excused**. The defence is available to professional and lay trustees, and has been successfully pleaded by professional trustees (**Perrins v Bellamy (1898)**), though the general approach appears to be that professional trustees will find it difficult successfully to claim the defence (**Bartlett v Barclay's Bank (1980)**). Note, the decision of Perrins v Bellamy (1898) pre-dates the Trustee Act 1925. This case was decided under what was s3, Judicial Trustees Act 1896, which was identical to s61, requiring the trustee to act honesty and reasonably so they might fairly be excused.

13.18   A recent attempt by a professional trustee to claim protection from s61 failed in the case of **Lloyds TSB Bank plc v Markandan & Uddin (2012)** where, though the trustee might have acted honestly, they had acted unreasonably with the consequence that they were not given the protection of the statute.

Beneficiary consent at common law

13.19   At common law, if a beneficiary consents to a breach of trust, then the trustee is protected. The beneficiary must be **fully informed** of all the circumstances of the proposed action and, further, the beneficiary must be exercising their **free will** in making an **independent judgment** (**Re Pauling (1963)**).

Section 62, Trustee Act 1925

13.20   Under s62, Trustee Act 1925, where the beneficiary either **instigates**, **requests**, or **consents in writing** to a proposed action, then the trustee might escape liability. If the beneficiary is found to have instigated a breach of trust, their interest can be **impounded**. This means the beneficiary cannot enjoy their interest until losses are made good. Impounding *generally* only works against the holder of a **life interest**.

Set-off

13.21   Where trustees make losses, but also make profits on another linked transaction, then they can offset the losses against the profits which are made. Therefore, in **Bartlett v Barclay's Bank (1980)**, the court permitted the trustee to offset losses made on one transaction against the profits made in another transaction. In Bartlett, the profits from one property investment were to be put into the second property investment which suffered significant losses. By allowing the trustee to offset, it reduced Barclay's liability.

Exclusion clauses

13.22   It is possible for a trust deed to contain an **exclusion clause** excluding or limiting the trustee's liability for breach of trust. In **Armitage v Nurse (1997)**, a clause excluding liability up to and including **gross negligence** was valid. Even reckless indifference as to whether payments from a trust fund were made in breach of trust will not be excluded when it comes to assessing the coverage of a trustee exclusion clause (**Sofer v SwissIndependent Trustees SA (2019)**). Consequently, the trustees were not liable.

Limitation periods

13.23   In all areas of law, claimants must bring their claim within a certain period of time. Section 21, Limitation Act 1980 provides a **six-year limitation period** for an action to recover trust property. However, this is subject to exceptions where there is **any fraud** or **fraudulent breach of trust** or for recovery of trust property or its proceeds in the trustee's possession which the trustee has converted to his use.

Remedies

13.24   A range of remedies is available to the beneficiary. They may be required to **restore the trust fund** where, for example, they have taken it and used it as their own, or the beneficiary may claim **equitable compensation to make good losses** which the trust fund has suffered. Alternatively, where the trustee has made unauthorized profits, the trustee can be required to hold profits made in breach of trust or fiduciary duty on **constructive trust** for the beneficiary, or the trustee can be made to **account for the profits** made as a personal remedy. These are discussed in more detail in chapter 14.

13.25   In addition to these remedies, the beneficiary may trace misappropriated trust property (see chapter 15), or sue an individual who meddles in trust affairs (see chapter 16) either by assisting in a breach of trust or by knowingly receiving trust property.

CHAPTER 14
FIDUCIARY DUTIES

Introduction

14.01   A fiduciary is someone who is in a relationship of trust and confidence with another owing that other person an **unswerving obligation of loyalty (Bristol & West BS v Mothew (1998))**.

14.02   In light of such a statement, it should be fairly obvious that **trustees are fiduciaries**; they owe a fiduciary obligation of loyalty to the beneficiary. However, other relationships might also amount to fiduciary relationships. For example, executors of an estate are fiduciaries, owing their duties to the beneficiaries under the estate; solicitors owe fiduciary duties to their clients and directors owe fiduciary duties to the company of which they are a director and may, in exceptional circumstances, owe fiduciary duties to shareholders (**Allen v Hyatt (1914)**; **Re Chez Nico Restaurants (1992)**).

14.03   When carrying out his obligations, a fiduciary is expected to be selfless; the interests of the principal must always come ahead of those of the beneficiary. In **Bray v Ford (1896)**, the House of Lords made it clear that the fiduciary must not place himself into a position where his interest and his duty conflict; it was, as Lord Herschell stated, an **inflexible rule**. However, in saying this, Lord Herschell was careful to state that a law which was too strict might be exposed to ridicule and there might be some circumstances where flexibility is required.

Content of fiduciary obligations

14.04   Though fiduciary duties are fluid and the content must change as the circumstances of society change, some things might be stated with confidence. A fiduciary is not permitted to **profit from his position** and **must not enter into a conflict of interest**. These might almost be regarded as fundamental elements of fiduciary obligations.

14.05   A fiduciary is in a conflicted position; as an individual he would seek to help himself, but as a fiduciary he should not. He should put the interests of the principal before himself. Therefore, fiduciary duties might be said to be there for preventative reasons; to stop the fiduciary if he is tempted either to make a profit at the expense of the principal or to enter into a basic conflict of interest. They encourage compliance with their obligations.

14.06   As indicated, trustees are also fiduciaries. Trustees are subject to trustee duties and fiduciary duties. Both sets of duties are binding on a trustee and operate to explain the liability of trustees.

What constitutes a breach of fiduciary duty?

14.07   The best way to understand how fiduciary duties might be breached is by using case examples. In **Keech v Sandford (1726)** a lease of Romford market was held on trust for a minor beneficiary. When the lease came up for renewal, the freeholder did not want to renew in favour of the minor. Therefore, the trustee obtained the lease for himself. Unfortunately, he was the one person who could not renew the lease; he put his self-interest before the duty owed to the beneficiary. The trustee was required to hold the lease on constructive trust for the minor beneficiary.

14.08   In **Brown v IRC (1964)**, a solicitor used client money to make loans at a profit. He was required to give that profit over to the clients. He was given custody of the client money and his duty was to see its safe custody. By making a profit with it, he placed his self-interest ahead of his duty to his clients.

14.09   However, perhaps the best case which demonstrates the operation of fiduciary obligations, and the harshness of the rule of fiduciary liability, is **Boardman v**

Phipps (1966).

Boardman v Phipps (1966)(HL)

14.10 The case of Boardman v Phipps concerned a family trust set up under the estate of Mr Phipps. The trust had a shareholding of 8,000 shares in a company. The trustees were Mrs Phipps (the widow), Mrs Noble (the married daughter of Mr & Mrs Phipps), and Mr Fox (an accountant). There were meant to be five beneficiaries, the widow, the daughter, and Mr & Mrs Phipps' three sons, only two of whom were alive at the material time (John and Tom). Mrs Phipps had a life interest, and the children had an interest in the remainder. The other main participant in the action was Mr Boardman, solicitor to the trust.

14.11 After a series of discussions, Tom Phipps and Mr Boardman went along to the shareholders' meeting of the company, principally to represent the interests of the trust. At this meeting, they discovered that the company, under the right management, could produce a healthy profit. When they returned from the meeting, they informed the trustees and other beneficiaries of this fact suggesting that the trust should purchase the other shares and make the changes. However, there were problems.

14.12 First, as already indicated, the trust fund had not received dividends for some time so did not have the cash to purchase the shares. Secondly, the trust fund did not have the power to purchase more shares due to a restriction in the trust deed. Thirdly, even if they had applied to court to vary that power, it was unlikely the court would have granted that power to the trustees.

14.13 In light of these problems, Tom Phipps and Mr Boardman purchased the shares in the company in their own name and set about making changes. The changes made were so significant that the company became profitable, and declared dividends which benefited the trust fund and, inevitably, Tom Phipps and Mr Boardman. Initially, everyone was happy because everyone benefited. The happiness did not last long. John

Phipps, the other brother, for reasons inappropriate to speculate about, elected to sue Mr Boardman for breach of fiduciary duty.

14.14 Recall that Mr Boardman was not a trustee, rather he was the solicitor to the trust. Nevertheless, he still had a fiduciary obligation towards the beneficiaries under the trust and it was these which, it was alleged by John Phipps, he had breached.

14.15 By a majority of 3-2, the House of Lords held that Mr Boardman was in breach of fiduciary duty. By purchasing the shares in the company, based on information which he gained in his fiduciary capacity, he put his self-interest ahead of his fiduciary duties. The majority held that he had received confidential information in a fiduciary capacity and that the conflict of interest had fettered his impartiality when it came to decision-making in relation to the trust. The minority, on the other hand, because of those matters identified at paragraph 14.12, above, found that there was no serious possibility of a conflict of interest and, consequently, that Mr Boardman should be permitted to keep his profits.

14.16 The HL indorsed the order made by the judge at first instance, Wilberforce J (as he then was), which stated that, first, Mr Boardman had to account for the profits which he made on the shares and, secondly, that he had to hold 5/18ths of his shares on constructive trust for John Phipps. The strange figure of 5/18ths was arrived at because under the terms of the original trust, the remainder was split between the children: 5/18ths each to the sons, and 3/18ths to the daughter.

14.17 The case of Boardman remains a controversial one, but it is an important case in the context of fiduciary duties and liability.

Remedies for breach of fiduciary duties

14.18 The remedies available for breach of fiduciary duty are an **account of profits** or the **constructive trust**. The former, an **account of profits**, **is a personal remedy**. This remedy requires the defendant personally to account for the profit which they made by payment of an equivalent sum to the victim. The remedy of account of profits does require the fiduciary to be solvent. On the other hand, the remedy of the **constructive trust, is a proprietary remedy**. Since the constructive trust is a remedy against the property, it does not require the fiduciary to be solvent. The constructive trust also allows the victim to take the benefit of an increase in value and, further, it permits the victim to trace to recover property if the profit made has been used in some other venture and become more valuable. The purpose of both remedies is to ensure that the fiduciary does not retain unlawfully obtained profit (**Parr v Keystone Healthcare Ltd (2019)(CA)**).

14.19 To explain the real meaning of the distinction between the two, it is useful to draw a case example. In **Attorney-General for Hong Kong v Reid (1994)(PC)**, Reid was a prosecutor in Hong Kong. He took payments from criminals to see that charges against them would be dropped. Reid used the payments received to purchase land in his native New Zealand. When Reid's wrongdoing was discovered, the Crown sought recovery of the payments made to him. The remedy might either have been an account of profits or a constructive trust. The PC awarded a constructive trust, allowing the Crown to claim the land which Reid had purchased, including allowing it to take the benefit of the increase in the value of the land. An account of profits would have given the Crown the money which he had been paid, $2.5m, and therefore allow Reid to keep its increase in value for himself, whereas the remedy of constructive trust stripped him of all his ill-gotten gains.

14.20 One of the main unresolved issues in remedies for breach of fiduciary duty was the circumstances in which each remedy might be awarded. That has caused much debate in recent cases.

14.21 The Court of Appeal in the case of **Sinclair v Versailles (2011)** did a lot to clarify the law stating that a constructive trust would be imposed where the fiduciary has misappropriated a pre-existing right or property of the principal. In contrast, an account of profit would be awarded where the principal had no pre-existing interest in the property obtained in breach of fiduciary duty. This followed an earlier CA case of **Lister v Stubbs (1890)** where the payment of a bribe had to be paid to the principal by account of profits. The CA in Sinclair, rejected the approach in Reid. It might have been thought that Sinclair settled the law, but not so. In **FHR European Ventures v Cedar Capital Partners (2014)**, the Supreme Court held that, whatever the circumstances of the breach, the principal is permitted the remedy of constructive trust.

14.22 Though this might now be relatively straightforward and reflect a more direct approach to fiduciary wrongdoing indicating that it will not be tolerated in any circumstances, it does seem rather inelegant to respond to every breach of fiduciary duty with a constructive trust. Nevertheless, given the decision is from the Supreme Court, it would appear conclusive.

Remuneration

14.23 Insofar as remuneration of fiduciaries is concerned, the courts indicate a willingness to award remuneration where the contribution made by the fiduciary is exceptional. In **Boardman v Phipps (1966)**, at first instance, Wilberforce J awarded Mr Boardman remuneration calculated on the 'liberal scale' given the skill and initiative which Mr Boardman had shown in turning the company concerned around and declaring a dividend. The decision of first instance on the remuneration point was indorsed by the House of Lords. Note, however, that the award of remuneration should not act as an encouragement to the fiduciary to breach his duties (**Guinness v Saunders (1990)**).

CHAPTER 15
TRACING TRUST PROPERTY

Introduction

15.01 Where trust property is taken by the trustee, equity allows the beneficiary to sue the trustee personally for breach of trust or, where the trustee does not have the money or is bankrupt, to claim the property, or its substitute, by **tracing**.

Terminology

15.02 It is important to distinguish between **following** and **tracing**. **Following** is the process of **identifying the original property** and returning it to the victim. However, if this cannot be done, then **tracing** is the process of allowing the victim to identify substituted property and claiming that property instead.

Requirements of equitable proprietary tracing

15.03 Here we are concerned with **tracing in equity**, but there is also **common law tracing**. However, the beneficiary cannot trace at common law because of the requirement that legal title is needed to trace at common law; the beneficiary has only equitable title, so must trace in equity. The requirements to trace in equity are:

a) Equitable proprietary interest in the property being traced; AND,

b) Fiduciary relationship.

(Re Diplock (1948)).

15.04 The equitable proprietary interest is a beneficial interest under a trust, or an interest under an estate, but other interests might also be covered.

15.05   Fiduciary relationship is broad and covers the relationship of trustee-beneficiary, executor-legatee, executor-next of kin (**Re Diplock (1948)**), director-company, solicitor-client (**Re Hallett's Estate (1880)**), and so on.

15.06   The **ability** to **trace in equity** is **lost in certain circumstances**.

15.07   The ability to trace in equity is lost where an asset is taken in breach of trust and sold to a **bona fide purchaser for value without notice** ('**Equity's Darling**'). Equity's Darling provides consideration unaware of a breach of trust. Therefore, the beneficiary cannot get the property back, but may trace into the proceeds of sale.

15.08   It is also not possible to trace in equity where the trust property is **dissipated**, such as where the trustee takes trust money in breach of trust and goes for dinner at a restaurant (**Re Diplock (1948)**).

15.09   The final circumstance in which equitable tracing will be defeated is if the court considers the claim **inequitable** (**Re Diplock (1948)**).

Benefits of equitable proprietary tracing

15.10   Where the claimant is able to do so, a claim in equitable tracing does have significant benefits. First, it gives the beneficiary priority status over other creditors. Secondly, they can claim the benefit of an increase in the value of any property purchased with the beneficiary's money and, thirdly, there is no statutory limitation period, though the claim is subject to the equitable doctrine of laches, ie, delay.

The tracing rules

15.11   The success or failure of tracing in equity is determined by the application of rules. The rules are technical, but examples are used throughout to demonstrate their application. Most of the rules are concerned with movements into and out of a bank account, though this is not the limit of tracing.

Tracing into unmixed funds

15.12   Unmixed funds are, obviously, those funds which have not been mixed; the trustee has not mixed his funds with the beneficiary's money, nor mixed it with the money of another beneficiary.

15.13   Such unmixed funds can simply be reclaimed.

15.14   Where money taken is used to purchase other property, the beneficiary can claim that property, including any increase in its value.

Tracing into mixed funds

15.15   Tracing into mixed funds is slightly more complex. The answer to the question will be determined by whether the beneficiary's funds are mixed with trustee's own money or the funds of another beneficiary.

Beneficiary funds mixed with trustee funds

15.16   Where the trustee has taken the beneficiary's funds and mixed them with his own funds in a bank account, certain rules operate when funds are withdrawn from the bank account.

15.17   The first is the **presumption of honesty (Re Hallett's Estate (1880))**. This rule states that **the trustee is deemed to spend his own money first**. As a presumption, it can be rebutted (**Re Oatway (1903)**). It might be rebutted where the trustee removes funds, purchases an asset, and then dissipates the remaining funds. The trustee would be dissipating his own funds. The presumption would not operate against the beneficiary.

15.18   In **Shalson v Russo (2003)** it was said that the beneficiary could **cherry pick** making a claim to more valuable assets which had been purchased, even though funds remained to meet the beneficiary's claim. This was not followed in **Turner v Jacob (2006)**. Both of these cases are High Court decisions so it would be open to a future court to choose between the two.

15.19 Where a trustee takes trust money from an account and spends it, then deposits his own money into the same account, this is not presumed to be a repayment to the trust fund unless the **trustee shows a clear intention to repay** (**Roscoe v Winder (1913)**). The most the beneficiary can claim is the **lowest intermediate balance**. If the account is emptied in the intermediate period, the beneficiaries cannot trace (**Bishopsgate Investment Management Ltd v Homan (1995)**).

Beneficiary funds mixed with another beneficiary's funds

15.20 In this scenario, the trustee has taken from two funds of which he is the trustee and mixed those two funds together, usually in a bank account. The first question to determine is what type of bank account: **current account** or **deposit (savings) account**.

15.21 If the funds are mixed in a **current account**, then the rule in **Clayton's Case (1816)** applies. This states that the first money into the account is the first money out ('**first in, first out**'). Thus, it depends on **when** the beneficiary money was placed in the account.

15.22 Given that 'first in, first out' hinges on an **accident of timing**, the case is criticised. In **Barlow Clowes International Ltd v Vaughan (1992)**, it was stated that 'first in, first out' would not be applied where:

a) it was contrary to the express or implied intentions of the claimants;

b) it was impractical; or

c) it would cause injustice.

15.23 Though probably still the default rule, it is more often disapplied (**Russell-Cooke Trust Co v Prentis (2002)**; **Charity Commission v Framjee (2014)**).

15.24 If the 'first in, first out' rule is displaced, the parties will share withdrawals rateably.

15.25 Where a deposit (savings) account, withdrawals are shared rateably between the beneficiaries.

Trust money used on property of an innocent volunteer

15.26 Where an innocent volunteer uses trust money, which they have been given, to improve their pre-owned asset, for example, by making improvements to their house, then the most the beneficiary would be able to claim is a charge to recover the amount taken from them, but even this would not be permitted if it would be inequitable (per Lord Browne-Wilkinson, obiter, **Foskett v McKeown (2001)**).

What can be claimed in mixed funds?

15.27 Where trust money or property has been mixed with other funds, the beneficiary *generally* has the right to an equitable charge (or lien) over the mixture (**Re Hallett's Estate (1880)**), or a claim to a proportion of the property corresponding to his own contribution (**Re Tilley's WT (1967)**). This was confirmed by **Foskett v McKeown (2001)**. The beneficiary should exercise the option in their favour.

Subrogation

15.28 Another possible remedy where an innocent volunteer uses the beneficiary's funds to pay off a **secured debt**, eg, a mortgage, is **subrogation**. 'Reviving' subrogation allows the beneficiary to bring the debt back to life and step into the shoes of the former mortgagee so long as the 'revived' mortgage is on the same terms as the original mortgage which was discharged (**Boscawen v Bajwa (1995)**).

Backwards Tracing

15.29   Backwards tracing is not permitted in English law at the moment. However, a recent decision of the Privy Council may have opened the door to the possibility in the future (**Brazil v Durant International Corporation (2015)**).

15.30   Backwards tracing is most easily explained by use of an example. Suppose I have £5,000 in my bank current account and I pay £6,000 for a car, the bank providing me with an overdraft of £1,000. In order to clear the overdraft, I steal £1,000 from the trust fund of which I am trustee. Under the usual principles of equitable tracing, the £1,000 would be regarded as dissipated (Re Diplock), so the beneficiary's claim would be defeated. However, the Privy Council now raises the possibility that the beneficiary may 'backwards trace' into the overdraft and claim an interest into the car which was purchased. Previously this would not have been permitted because the beneficiary had no proprietary interest in the funds used to purchase the car. In the future, it may be possible.

The Diplock personal action

15.31   The personal Diplock action (or personal Diplock claim) is **available only to the legatee under an estate, not a beneficiary under a trust**. It gives the legatee under an estate the right to sue, personally, any recipient of estate property. The right is a personal action and not defeated by dissipation of the asset.

15.32   The legatee must sue the personal representative under the estate in the first instance, and if that claim fails, then the personal Diplock action is available. The claim is limited to the sum overpaid, with no interest.

15.33   Importantly, there is no defence to the claim, but in the future the **defence** of **change of position** *may* be available. The change of position defence comes from **Lipkin**

Gorman v Karpnale (1991) and applies where the recipient spends money in good faith in reliance on the payment received and, further, that the expenditure was unusual or extraordinary.

CHAPTER 16
LIABILITY OF STRANGERS

Introduction

16.01   A stranger is someone who is not appointed a trustee, yet they interfere in trust affairs when they should not do.

16.02   The liability of a stranger is personal, ie, it attaches to them personally; this is unlike equitable tracing which is proprietary.

Trustee de son tort

16.03   The category of the 'trutee de son tort' ('trustee of his own wrong') is a narrow category and not one which has a huge significance in modern trusts law. The trustee de son tort undertakes the tasks of a trustee, even though he is not appointed a trustee. An example would be the personal assistant of a trustee performing certain trustee functions while the trustee is out of the country and where this has not been officially delegated to them. The trustee de son tort will be personally liable for any losses (**Mara v Browne (1895)**).

Strangers liability

16.04   The main forms of strangers liability in modern trusts law are **knowing receipt** and **dishonest assistance** (per Lord Selbourne, LC, in **Barnes v Addy (1874)**).

Terminology

16.05   Before explaining knowing receipt and dishonest assistance, it is wise to clarify the terminology. You may find the expression in books and cases that the liability of strangers is the 'liability to account as a constructive trustee'. This can lead to confusion because of the use of 'constructive trustee' which can lead some to think that liability is proprietary. This is not the case. **The liability of a stranger is personal.** What the phrase 'liability to account as a constructive trustee' means is that the stranger is made liable to account *as if* they were a trustee. Of course, the liability of a trustee is personal.

Knowing Receipt

16.06   The cause of action in knowing receipt requires:

a)   Disposal of the claimant's assets in breach of fiduciary duty;

b)   Beneficial receipt by the defendant of assets which are traceable as representing the claimant's assets;

c)   Knowledge on the part of the defendant that the assets received are traceable to a breach of fiduciary duty.

(El Ajou v Dollar Land Holdings plc (1994))

16.07   The third element has caused most difficulties in the cases. Famously **Baden, Delvaux and Lecuit v Société Générale pour Favoriser le Développement du Commerce et de l'Industrie en France SA (1983)** – (Re Baden, for short), provided five categories of knowledge:

i) Actual knowledge;

ii) Wilfully closing one's eyes to the obvious (A recent example of which can be found in the case of **Group Seven Ltd v Notable Services LLP (2019)(CA)**);

iii) Wilfully and recklessly failing to make such inquiries as an honest and reasonable man would make;

iv) Knowledge of circumstances which would indicate the facts to an honest and reasonable man;

v) Knowledge of circumstances which would put an honest and reasonable man on inquiry.

16.08 However, the CA in **Bank of Credit and Commerce International (Overseas) Ltd and another v Akindele (2000)** stated that the recipient's state of knowledge had to be such as to make it **unconscionable for him to retain the benefit of the receipt**. This is now the position in law.

16.09 The approach in Akindele was confirmed by CA in **City Index v Gawler (2007)** and the High Court in **Starglade v Nash (2009)**. It was also confirmed in **Armstrong v Winnington Networks (2012)**, though the judge in the case, something with which counsel for both parties agreed, used the Baden categories of knowledge in order to reach a decision. See, also, **Group Seven Ltd v Nasir (2017)**. So, the Re Baden categories of knowledge may have some continuing use in determining whether the circumstances are unconscionable or not.

16.10 At the moment, liability for knowing receipt is based on fault. However, some have suggested that liability should be **strict** but **subject to** the **change of position defence** (Nicholls, Knowing Receipt: The Need for a New Landmark, in, Jones and Cornish (eds), Restitution: Past, Present and Future (1998)), though this approach was doubted by Nourse LJ in Akindele.

16.11 The correctness of the unconscionability test was recently confirmed by the cases of **Keown v Nahoor (2015)**, **Glenn v Watson and Others (2018)**, and **FM Capital Partners Ltd v Marino & Ors (2018)**.

Dishonest Assistance

16.12 The law on dishonest assistance has caused significantly greater problems for the judiciary than the law on knowing receipt. The problems centered on the test of dishonesty to be used for the claim.

16.13   The cause of action requires:

a)   A trust or other fiduciary relationship;

b)   A breach of trust or fiduciary duty;

c)   Assistance by the stranger in that breach of trust or fiduciary duty;

d)   Dishonesty on the part of the accessory.

(Re Baden (1983))

16.14   As indicated, the problems have been created over the fourth element; the test of dishonesty applicable to the accessory. The starting point is the Privy Council case of **Royal Brunei Airlines v Tan (1995)**.

16.15   In Tan, Lord Nicholls did much to clarify the law, stating that dishonesty was necessary for the cause of action and, further, that it was the accessory who needed to be dishonest; the honesty or otherwise of the trustee was not relevant.

16.16   The **test of dishonesty is an objective one**; the accessory was to be judged by the standards of reasonable and honest men. **Did the defendant fall below the standards of the reasonable man?** Though the test is an objective one, limited account might be taken of the characteristics of the defendant, eg, his experience, his qualifications, his professional status, and so on. However, the **test of dishonesty is objective**.

16.17   Tan was not the final word on the issue. In **Twinsectra Ltd v Yardley (2002)**, the HL appeared to change the law. Their Lordships adopted the 'combined' test of dishonesty used in criminal law (**R v Ghosh (1982)**). This asks two question: one objective, one subjective. **Was the defendant's conduct dishonest by the standards of reasonable and honest people? AND did the defendant realise that by his conduct he was dishonest?** The first limb is objective, but the second limb is subjective.

16.18 The adoption of a criminal standard in a civil matter was not welcome and Twinsectra received significant criticism. The retreat from Twinsectra did not take long.

16.19 The PC in **Barlow Clowes International Ltd v Eurotrust International Ltd (2005)** reinterpreted Twinsectra as a **purely objective test** – something which it plainly was not. Nevertheless, this change was welcomed. However, Twinsectra is HL and, technically, still binding on courts in England and Wales. This might have created some problems but for a further piece of judicial ingenuity in the CA case of **Abou-Rahmah v Abacha (2006)** where it was stated that the test of dishonesty binding in England and Wales was Twinsectra *as interpreted in* Barlow Clowes. Though this is not ideal, it at least means that an objective test is applied to cases of dishonest assistance. The approach of Abou-Rahmah was followed by CA in **Starglade Properties Ltd v Nash (2010)** and HC in **Pulvers v Chan (2007)** and **Aerostar Maintenance International Ltd v Wilson (2010)**.

16.20 In reviewing the civil law for dishonesty, though not in the dishonest assistance context, in the recent case of **Ivey v Genting Casinos (UK) Ltd (2017)**, the Supreme Court stated that the law on dishonest assistance is now settled as being represented by **Royal Brunei Airlines v Tan (1995)** and **Barlow Clowes International Ltd v Eurotrust International Ltd (2005)**: see, Lord Hughes, paras 62 and 74. Though these comments might only be regarded as obiter, the line is being picked up and used by judges (**Signia Wealth Ltd v Vector Trustees Ltd & Ors (2018)**).

CHAPTER 17
EQUITABLE REMEDIES

Introduction

17.01   At common law damages is the remedy of right, but in some circumstances damages will not satisfy the claimant; the claimant will want the thing they contracted for. If so, the claimant will need to convince the court that they are entitled to an equitable remedy.

17.02   Equitable remedies are those remedies that were traditionally awarded by the Chancery Court. They are available where damages would prove an inadequate remedy (**Adderley v Dixon (1824)**) and they are only available at the discretion of the court. In other words, the claimant must convince the court that only an equitable remedy will satisfy the claim.

17.03   In the context of contract claims, the main equitable remedies are **specific performance** and the **injunction.**

Specific Performance

17.04   Specific performance is a court order compelling a party to perform their positive obligations under a contract. Generally, when determining the principles applicable for the award of specific performance, it is necessary to determine whether the contract is one for the sale of goods or a contract for the provision of services.

17.05   In a **contract for the sale of goods**, generally the court asks whether the item contracted for has a **quality of uniqueness** about it. Note, it does not have to be the only one, but merely to have a quality of uniqueness which makes the item difficult to obtain elsewhere.

17.06   In **Falcke v Gray (1859)** Ming vases were

sufficiently unique, while in **Cohen v Roche (1927)**, Hepplewhite chairs were not. If the item has been modified to meet the claimant's specific needs, then specific performance is more likely to be granted (**Behnke v Bede Shipping Co Ltd (1927)**). That said, a contract for a commonly available commodity might be enforced if its availability is limited at time because of strike action (**Sky Petroleum v VIP Petroleum Ltd (1974)**).

17.07   Insofar as contracts for services are concerned, employment contracts cannot be specifically enforced (**s236, Trade Union and Labour Relations (Consolidation) Act 1992**), but contracts for services may be specifically enforced in some circumstances (**Giles & Co Ltd v Morris (1972)**), though these circumstances need to be exceptional (**LauritzenCool AB v Lady Navigation Inc (2005)**).

17.08   If the contract requires an onerous level of **supervision**, the courts are reluctant to grant specific performance (**Ryan v Mutual Tontine Westminster Chambers Association (1893)**), unless the contract defines the obligations clearly so monitoring compliance is simple (**Posner v Scott-Lewis (1987)**). In **Co-operative Insurance Society Ltd v Argyll Stores (Holdings) Ltd (1997)**, HL refused specific performance of a lease of a supermarket premises in a shopping centre since the court was reluctant to be called upon to intervene by a series of actions in contempt proceedings to enforce any order.

17.09   If there are difficulties in obtaining an alternative supplier of the services at short notice, then the courts might be more inclined to specific performance (**Verrall v Great Yarmouth BC (1981)**).

17.10   A claimant should not unduly delay an application for **specific performance** as claims may be barred under the equitable doctrine of **laches** (delay).

Injunctions

17.11 Where time is of the essence in a contract, specific performance is not the best remedy since it is only available at full trial. Consequently, the claimant might seek an **interim mandatory injunction** which is available at an early stage in the litigation. An interim mandatory injunction is a court order compelling the defendant to act in a particular way. It would have the same effect as an order for specific performance, only at an earlier stage in litigation. To obtain one, the claimant must give the court a high degree of assurance that it will turn out at full trial to have been correctly awarded at the early stage (**Shepherd Homes v Sandham (1970)**). This is usually achieved by relying on the principles applicable to specific performance, above. Note, however, that the interim mandatory injunction is not a remedy which is specific to contract.

17.12 As an alternative before a hearing, the claimant might seek and **interim prohibitory injunction**. This would prevent the other contracting party from selling the subject-matter of the contract to someone else. An interim prohibitory injunction is obtained using the American Cyanamid Guidelines from **American Cyanamid v Ethicon Ltd (1975)**. The claimant has to show:

a) Whether there is a **serious question to be tried**;

b) Whether the **balance of convenience** favours the grant of the order;

c) If the balance of convenience is even, then the **status quo ante** applies. This is the position before the change of circumstances and *generally* favours the claimant;

d) Special factors. This permits the court to consider any circumstances relevant to the application.

17.13   It is worth bearing in mind, that these are *guidelines*, not rules. Therefore, in applying the guidelines the courts are afforded a high degree of flexibility. Further, an interim prohibitory injunction is not limited to contractual claims, but might operate to prevent a nuisance, or a threatened breach of trust.

17.14   It is worth noting that in the Privy Council decision of **National Commercial Bank Jamaica v Olint (2009)**, Lord Hoffmann stated that the argument about whether an injunction should be classified as mandatory or prohibitory was a redundant argument. Though only Privy Council, the argument did receive some traction in the High Court case of **Atlas Residential Solutions Management UK Ltd v Greengate SARL (2019)**.

Freezing Order

17.15   This is a type of prohibitory injunction. It operates to prevent the defendant from dealing with their assets before a trial.

17.16   A freezing order is obtained by the claimant demonstrating:

   a)   A good arguable case;

   b)   Defendant has assets within the jurisdiction;

   c)   Current and real risk of removal or dissipation of assets by the defendant (**Ivy Technology v Martin (2019)**). Note, an actual risk of dissipation is not required (**Al Jaber v Bosheh (2019)**).

17.17   These injunctions are *usually* applied for **without notice**. This means only the claimant is present at the hearing. This is unusual for English law.

17.18   To support the freezing order, the court may order a disclosure order requiring the defendant to disclose their assets. This is known as a 'Shapira Order'.

17.19 A freezing order might also be extra-territorial (**Re BCCI SA (No 9)**). This means the order can prevent the defendant dealing with their assets overseas.

Search Order

17.20 A search order is a mandatory injunction compelling the defendant to allow the claimant access to their property for the purposes of discovering documentation and other evidence of which there is risk of destruction by the defendant.

17.21 To obtain a search order, the claimant must satisfy three conditions:

a)   An extremely strong prima facie case;

b)   Very serious damage, potential or actual, to the claimant;

c)   Clear evidence the defendant has incriminating documents or other property in his possession and that there is a real possibility of destruction.

17.22 The search order is always without notice. This is because of the risk that should the defendant learn of the application, they are likely to destroy evidence so the order, if granted, could not properly be executed.

17.23 There are certain safeguards concerning the award of a search order:

a)   Order served in presence of an independent 'supervising solicitor' who is able to explain the process to the defendant;

b)   Entry should take place between 9.30 am and 5.30 pm to allow the defendant the opportunity to seek legal advice;

c)   Search must take place in defendant's presence;

d)   A record of items removed must be made and presented to the defendant;

126

e) Where defendant is female, one of the party executing the search order should be female.

17.24 If the defendant is not at the premises, the order cannot be carried out. Remember, it is an order against the defendant so the defendant will need to be present.

17.25 In **Chappell v United Kingdom (1990)**, a human rights breach challenge to search orders failed.

Account of Profits

17.26 An account of profits is available against a defendant who profits from a breach of trust or an obligation of confidence. This requires them to give up profits which they might have made from the breach.

Rescission

17.27 Rescission is the right to have a contract set aside, usually where a misrepresentation has been committed.

Rectification

17.28 This remedy permits a written contract to be modified where it does not reflect the agreement reached between the parties. It is very narrow in its scope.

Defences to Equitable Remedies

17.29 A claimant seeking equitable remedies must have clean hands, ie, must have behaved well before seeking the remedy claimed (**Coatsworth v Johnson (1886)**). Further, the claimant must not unduly delay since delay defeats equity (**Eads v Williams (1854)**). Since equity does seek to temper the harshness of the common law, an equitable remedy will not be granted where to do so would be unduly harsh to the defendant (**Patel v Ali (1984)**), though this will be reviewed on a case by case basis and hardship will not always, automatically, act as a defence (**Shah v Greening (2016)**).

ABOUT THE AUTHOR

I'm a law lecturer with over 20 years' experience of teaching and explaining the law at undergraduate and postgraduate levels. I have tutored students in both the public and private sectors, at old and new universities, across a range of subjects, including equity and trusts law.

Printed in Great Britain
by Amazon